THE
PSALMS

for
TODAY

Today's English Version

THE
PSALMS

for
TODAY

Today's English Version

AMERICAN BIBLE SOCIETY
New York

THE PSALMS

in Today's English Version

The Psalms were originally published as

PSALMS FOR MODERN MAN

ENG. PSALMS TEV560P
ABS-1980-60,000-5,965,000-We-28-4R-04456

PREFACE

THE BOOK OF PSALMS is the hymnbook and prayer book of the Bible. Composed by different authors over a long period of time, these hymns and prayers were collected and used by the people of Israel in their worship, and eventually this collection was included in their Holy Scriptures.

These religious poems are of many kinds: there are hymns of praise and worship of God; prayers for help, protection, and salvation; pleas for forgiveness; songs of thanksgiving for God's blessings; and petitions for the punishment of enemies. These prayers are personal and national; some portray the most intimate feelings of one person, while others represent the needs and feelings of all the people of God.

Many of the Psalms are quoted in the New Testament, and such passages as Mary's song of praise (Luke 1.46-55), Zechariah's prophecy (Luke 1.68-79), and Simeon's prayer of thanksgiving (Luke 2.29-32) reflect the language and style of the psalms. They were used by Jesus, quoted by the writers of the New Testament, and became the treasured book of worship of the Christian Church from its very beginning.

This translation of *The Psalms* attempts to represent the meaning of the Hebrew text as faithfully as possible, and at the same time convey something of the grace and beauty of the original poetry. The basic poetic structure of the Psalms consists of a statement which is repeated, in a modified fashion, in the next line. Sometimes this parallelism is continued over several lines. The possible variations are almost unlimited, and the reader who is aware of them will discover new beauty in the Psalms. In addition, unusual words and figurative expressions help create and sustain a poetic atmosphere.

Ancient Hebrew poetry did not have rhyme, and the meter was quite different from what is commonly used in English. This translation has been made in free verse, and the translators have tried to put the Psalms in easy-flowing, rhythmical lines that can be effective in public worship as well as in private devotion.

Today's English Version is a distinctively new translation, which does not conform to traditional vocabulary or style. It seeks instead to express the meaning of the Hebrew text in words and forms accepted as standard by people everywhere who employ English as a means of communication.

Where there is general agreement that the Hebrew text presents unresolved difficulties in interpretation, this translation employs the evidence of other ancient texts or follows present-day scholarly concensus. All such modifications are identified in footnotes. Other footnotes give information designed to help the reader understand the meaning of the text, especially where ancient beliefs are expressed or alluded to.

The Bible in Today's English Version is called the *Good News Bible* and is available from the American Bible Society.

THE PSALMS

Outline of Contents

The 150 psalms are grouped into five collections, or books, as follows:

BOOK ONE
(Psalms 1—41)

True Happiness

1 Happy are those
   who reject the advice of evil men,
who do not follow the example of
   sinners
   or join those who have no use for
   God.
2 Instead, they find joy in obeying the
   Law of the LORD,
   and they study it day and night.
3 They are like trees that grow beside a
   stream,
   that bear fruit at the right time,
   and whose leaves do not dry up.
They succeed in everything they do.

4 But evil men are not like this at all;
   they are like straw that the wind
   blows away.
5 Sinners will be condemned by God
   and kept apart from God's own
   people.
6 The righteous are guided and protected
   by the LORD,
   but the evil are on the way to their
   doom.

1

God's Chosen King

2 Why do the nations plan rebellion?
   Why do people make their useless
     plots?

2 Their kings revolt,
    their rulers plot together against the
      LORD
    and against the king he chose.
3 "Let us free ourselves from their rule,"
     they say;
    "let us throw off their control."

4 From his throne in heaven the Lord
     laughs
    and mocks their feeble plans.
5 Then he warns them in anger
    and terrifies them with his fury.
6 "On Zion,[a] my sacred hill," he says,
    "I have installed my king."

7 "I will announce," says the king, "what
     the LORD has declared.
    He said to me: 'You are my son;
    today I have become your father.
8 Ask, and I will give you all the nations;
    the whole earth will be yours.
9 You will break them with an iron rod;
    you will shatter them in pieces like a
      clay pot.' "

10 Now listen to this warning, you kings;
    learn this lesson, you rulers of the
      world:
11 Serve the LORD with fear;
    tremble 12 and bow down to him;[b]

---

[a] ZION: *The term "Zion" (originally a designation for "David's City,"
the Jebusite stronghold captured by King David's forces) was later
extended in meaning to refer to the hill on which the Temple stood.*
[b] *Probable text* tremble ... him; *some other possible texts* with
trembling kiss his feet *and* with trembling kiss the Son *and* tremble
and kiss the mighty one; *Hebrew unclear.*

or else his anger will be quickly
  aroused,
    and you will suddenly die.
Happy are all who go to him for
  protection.

Morning Prayer for Help[c]

3 I have so many enemies, LORD,
    so many who turn against me!
[2] They talk about me and say,
    "God will not help him."

[3] But you, O LORD, are always my shield
    from danger;
  you give me victory
  and restore my courage.

You, O LORD, are always my shield from danger. (3.3)

[4] I call to the LORD for help,
    and from his sacred hill[d] he answers
    me.

[c] HEBREW TITLE: *A psalm by David, after he ran away from his son Absalom.*   [d] SACRED HILL: *See 2.6.*

⁵ I lie down and sleep,
  and all night long the LORD protects
    me.
⁶ I am not afraid of the thousands of
    enemies
  who surround me on every side.

⁷ Come, LORD! Save me, my God!
  You punish all my enemies
    and leave them powerless to harm
      me.
⁸ Victory comes from the LORD—
  may he bless his people.

Evening Prayer for Help *

4 Answer me when I pray,
    O God, my defender!
  When I was in trouble, you helped me.
    Be kind to me now and hear my
      prayer.

² How long will you people insult me?
    How long will you love what is
      worthless
    and go after what is false?

³ Remember that the LORD has chosen
    the righteous for his own,
  and he hears me when I call to him.

⁴ Tremble with fear and stop sinning;
    think deeply about this,
    when you lie in silence on your beds.
⁵ Offer the right sacrifices to the LORD,
    and put your trust in him.

⁶ There are many who pray:
    "Give us more blessings, O LORD.
    Look on us with kindness!"
⁷ But the joy that you have given me
    is more than they will ever have
    with all their grain and wine.

---

* HEBREW TITLE: *A psalm by David.*

8 When I lie down, I go to sleep in peace;
   you alone, O Lord, keep me
   perfectly safe.

A Prayer for Protection *f*

5 Listen to my words, O Lord,
   and hear my sighs.
2 Listen to my cry for help,
   my God and king!

I pray to you, O Lord;
3   you hear my voice in the morning;
at sunrise I offer my prayer *g*
   and wait for your answer.

4 You are not a God who is pleased with
      wrongdoing;
   you allow no evil in your presence.
5 You cannot stand the sight of proud
      men;
   you hate all wicked people.
6 You destroy all liars
   and despise violent, deceitful men.

7 But because of your great love
   I can come into your house;
I can worship in your holy Temple
   and bow down to you in reverence.
8 Lord, I have so many enemies!
   Lead me to do your will;
   make your way plain for me to
      follow.

9 What my enemies say can never be
      trusted;
   they only want to destroy.
Their words are flattering and smooth,
   but full of deadly deceit.
10 Condemn and punish them, O God;
   may their own plots cause their ruin.

---

f HEBREW TITLE: *A psalm by David.*   *g* prayer; *or* sacrifice.

Drive them out of your presence
because of their many sins
and their rebellion against you.

11 But all who find safety in you will
rejoice;
they can always sing for joy.
Protect those who love you;
because of you they are truly happy.
12 You bless those who obey you, LORD;
your love protects them like a shield.

A Prayer for Help in Time of Trouble[h]

6 LORD, don't be angry and rebuke
me!
Don't punish me in your anger!
2 I am worn out, O LORD; have pity on
me!
Give me strength; I am completely
exhausted
3   and my whole being is deeply
troubled.
How long, O LORD, will you wait to
help me?

4 Come and save me, LORD;
in your mercy rescue me from death.
5 In the world of the dead you are not
remembered;
no one can praise you there.

6 I am worn out with grief;
every night my bed is damp from my
weeping;
my pillow is soaked with tears.
7 I can hardly see;
my eyes are so swollen
from the weeping caused by my
enemies.

[h] HEBREW TITLE: *A psalm by David.*

⁸ Keep away from me, you evil men!
  The LORD hears my weeping;
⁹   he listens to my cry for help
  and will answer my prayer.
¹⁰ My enemies will know the bitter shame
        of defeat;
      in sudden confusion they will be
        driven away.

A Prayer for Justice[i]

7 O LORD, my God, I come to you for
        protection;
  rescue me and save me from all who
        pursue me,
² or else like a lion they will carry me off
  where no one can save me,
  and there they will tear me to pieces.

³⁻⁴ O LORD, my God, if I have wronged
        anyone,
  if I have betrayed a friend
  or without cause done violence to my
        enemy[j]
  if I have done any of these things—
⁵ then let my enemies pursue me and
        catch me,
  let them cut me down and kill me
  and leave me lifeless on the ground!

⁶ Rise in your anger, O LORD!
  Stand up against the fury of my
        enemies;
  rouse yourself and help me!
  Justice is what you demand,
⁷   so bring together all the peoples
        around you,
  and rule over them from above.[k]

[i] HEBREW TITLE: *A song which David sang to the LORD because of
Cush the Benjaminite.*   [j] *without cause done violence to my enemy;
or* shown mercy to someone who wronged me unjustly.
[k] *Probable text* rule over them from above; *Hebrew* return above
over them.

⁸ You are the judge of all mankind.
   Judge in my favor, O LORD;
   you know that I am innocent.
⁹ You are a righteous God
   and judge our thoughts and desires.
   Stop the wickedness of evil men
   and reward those who are good.

¹⁰ God is my protector;
   he saves those who obey him.
¹¹ God is a righteous judge
   and always condemns the wicked.
¹² If they do not change their ways,
   God will sharpen his sword.
   He bends his bow and makes it ready;
¹³   he takes up his deadly weapons
   and aims his burning arrows.

¹⁴ See how wicked people think up evil;
   they plan trouble and practice
      deception.
¹⁵ But in the traps they set for others,
   they themselves get caught.
¹⁶ So they are punished by their own evil
   and are hurt by their own violence.

¹⁷ I thank the LORD for his justice;
   I sing praises to the LORD, the Most
      High.

God's Glory and Man's Dignity*

8 O LORD, our Lord,
   your greatness is seen in all the
      world!
   Your praise reaches up to the heavens;
²   it is sung by children and babies.
   You are safe and secure from all your
      enemies;
   you stop anyone who opposes you.

*HEBREW TITLE: *A psalm by David.*

Your greatness is seen in all the world! (8.9)

³ When I look at the sky, which you have
        made,
    at the moon and the stars, which you
        set in their places—
⁴ what is man, that you think of him;
    mere man, that you care for him?

⁵ Yet you made him inferior only to
        yourself;ᵐ
    you crowned him with glory and
        honor.
⁶ You appointed him ruler over
        everything you made;
    you placed him over all creation:
⁷   sheep and cattle, and the wild
        animals too;
⁸   the birds and the fish
    and the creatures in the seas.

⁹ O LORD, our Lord,
    your greatness is seen in all the
        world!

ᵐ yourself; *or* the gods, *or* the angels.

Thanksgiving to God for His Justice[n]

9 I will praise you, LORD, with all my
    heart;
I will tell of all the wonderful things
    you have done.
2 I will sing with joy because of you.
    I will sing praise to you, Almighty
        God.

3 My enemies turn back when you
    appear;
they fall down and die.
4 You are fair and honest in your
    judgments,
and you have judged in my favor.

5 You have condemned the heathen
    and destroyed the wicked;
they will be remembered no more.
6 Our enemies are finished forever;
    you have destroyed their cities,
    and they are completely forgotten.

7 But the LORD is king forever;
    he has set up his throne for judgment.
8 He rules the world with righteousness;
    he judges the nations with justice.

9 The LORD is a refuge for the oppressed,
    a place of safety in times of trouble.
10 Those who know you, LORD, will trust
    you;
you do not abandon anyone who
    comes to you.

11 Sing praise to the LORD, who rules in
    Zion!
Tell every nation what he has done!

[n] HEBREW TITLE: *A psalm by David.*

12 God remembers those who suffer;
   he does not forget their cry,
   and he punishes those who wrong
      them.

13 Be merciful to me, O LORD!
   See the sufferings my enemies cause
      me!
   Rescue me from death, O LORD,
14   that I may stand before the people of
      Jerusalem
   and tell them all the things for which
      I praise you.
   I will rejoice because you saved me.

15 The heathen have dug a pit and fallen
      in;
   they have been caught in their own
      trap.
16 The LORD has revealed himself by his
      righteous judgments,
   and the wicked are trapped by their
      own deeds.

17 Death is the destiny of all the wicked,
   of all those who reject God.
18 The needy will not always be neglected;
   the hope of the poor will not be
      crushed forever.

19 Come, LORD! Do not let men defy you!
   Bring the heathen before you
   and pronounce judgment on them.
20 Make them afraid, O LORD;
   make them know that they are only
      mortal beings.

A Prayer for Justice

10 Why are you so far away, O
      LORD?
   Why do you hide yourself when we
      are in trouble?

2 The wicked are proud and persecute
   the poor;
  catch them in the traps they have
    made.

3 The wicked man is proud of his evil
   desires;
  the greedy man curses and rejects the
   LORD.
4 A wicked man does not care about the
   LORD;
  in his pride he thinks that God
   doesn't matter.

5 A wicked man succeeds in everything.
  He cannot understand God's
   judgments;
  he sneers at his enemies.
6 He says to himself, "I will never fail;
  I will never be in trouble."
7 His speech is filled with curses, lies,
   and threats;
  he is quick to speak hateful, evil
   words.

8 He hides himself in the villages,
  waiting to murder innocent people.
  He spies on his helpless victims;
9   he waits in his hiding place like a
   lion.
  He lies in wait for the poor;
  he catches them in his trap and drags
   them away.

10 The helpless victims lie crushed;
  brute strength has defeated them.
11 The wicked man says to himself, "God
   doesn't care!
  He has closed his eyes and will never
   see me!"

¹² O Lord, punish those wicked men!
    Remember those who are suffering!
¹³ How can a wicked man despise God
    and say to himself, "He will not
        punish me"?

¹⁴ But you do see; you take notice of
        trouble and suffering
    and are always ready to help.
The helpless man commits himself to
        you;
    you have always helped the needy.

¹⁵ Break the power of wicked and evil
        men;
    punish them for the wrong they have
        done
    until they do it no more.

¹⁶ The Lord is king forever and ever.
    Those who worship other gods
    will vanish from his land.

¹⁷ You will listen, O Lord, to the prayers
        of the lowly;
    you will give them courage.
¹⁸ You will hear the cries of the oppressed
        and the orphans;
    you will judge in their favor,
    so that mortal men may cause terror
        no more.

Confidence in the Lord⁰

11 I trust in the Lord for safety.
    How foolish of you to say to
        me,
"Fly away like a bird to the mountains,ᵖ

⁰ HEBREW TITLE: *By David.* ᵖ *Some ancient translations* like a bird
to the mountains; *Hebrew* bird, to your *(plural)* mountains.

2   because the wicked have drawn their
  bows and aimed their arrows
to shoot from the shadows at good
  men.
3 There is nothing a good man can do
  when everything falls apart."

4 The LORD is in his holy temple;
  he has his throne in heaven.
He watches people everywhere
  and knows what they are doing.
5 He examines the good and the wicked
  alike;
  the lawless he hates with all his heart.

6 He sends down flaming coals*a* and
  burning sulfur on the wicked;
he punishes them with scorching
  winds.
7 The LORD is righteous and loves good
  deeds;
  those who do them will live in his
  presence.

A Prayer for Help*r*

12 Help us, LORD!
  There is not a good man left;
  honest men can no longer be found.
2 All of them lie to one another;
  they deceive each other with flattery.

3 Silence those flattering tongues, O
  LORD!
  Close those boastful mouths that say,
4 "With our words we get what we want.
  We will say what we wish,
  and no one can stop us."

---

a One ancient translation coals; *Hebrew* traps. *r* HEBREW TITLE: *A
psalm by David.*

[5] "But now I will come," says the LORD,
   "because the needy are oppressed
   and the persecuted groan in pain.
I will give them the security they long
   for."

[6] The promises of the LORD can be
      trusted;
   they are as genuine as silver
   refined seven times in the furnace.

[7-8] Wicked men are everywhere,
   and everyone praises what is evil.
Keep us always safe, O LORD,
   and preserve us from such people.

A Prayer for Help[s]

13 How much longer will you forget
      me, LORD? Forever?
How much longer will you hide
   yourself from me?
[2] How long must I endure trouble?
   How long will sorrow fill my heart
      day and night?
   How long will my enemies triumph
      over me?

[3] Look at me, O LORD my God, and
      answer me.
   Restore my strength; don't let me die.
[4] Don't let my enemies say, "We have
      defeated him."
   Don't let them gloat over my
      downfall.

[5] I rely on your constant love;
   I will be glad, because you will
      rescue me.
[6] I will sing to you, O LORD,
   because you have been good to me.

[s] HEBREW TITLE: *A psalm by David.*

The Wickedness of Men[t]
(Psalm 53)

14 Fools say to themselves,
    "There is no God!"
They are all corrupt,
    and they have done terrible things;
    there is no one who does what is
      right.

2 The Lord looks down from heaven at
      mankind
    to see if there are any who are wise,
    any who worship him.
3 But they have all gone wrong;
    they are all equally bad.
Not one of them does what is right,
    not a single one.

4 "Don't they know?" asks the Lord.
    "Are all these evildoers ignorant?
They live by robbing my people,
    and they never pray to me."

5 But then they will be terrified,
    for God is with those who obey him.
6 Evildoers frustrate the plans of the
      humble man,
    but the Lord is his protection.

7 How I pray that victory
    will come to Israel from Zion.
How happy the people of Israel will be
    when the Lord makes them
      prosperous again!

What God Requires[u]

15 Lord, who may enter your
      Temple?
Who may worship on Zion, your
    sacred hill?[v]

---

[t] HEBREW TITLE: *By David.*   [u] HEBREW TITLE: *A psalm by David.*
[v] SACRED HILL: *See 2.6.*

2 A person who obeys God in everything
   and always does what is right,
whose words are true and sincere,
3   and who does not slander others.
He does no wrong to his friends
   nor spreads rumors about his
      neighbors.
4 He despises those whom God rejects,
   but honors those who obey the LORD.
He always does what he promises,
   no matter how much it may cost.
5 He makes loans without charging
      interest
   and cannot be bribed to testify
      against the innocent.

Whoever does these things will always
   be secure.

A Prayer of Confidence[w]

16 Protect me, O God; I trust in you
      for safety.
2 I say to the LORD, "You are my Lord;
   all the good things I have come from
      you."

3 How excellent are the LORD's faithful
      people!
   My greatest pleasure is to be with
      them.

4 Those who rush to other gods
   bring many troubles on themselves.[x]
I will not take part in their sacrifices;
   I will not worship their gods.

5 You, LORD, are all I have,
   and you give me all I need;
   my future is in your hands.

---

[w] HEBREW TITLE: *A psalm by David.*   [x] *Probable text* Those . . .
themselves; *Hebrew unclear.*

⁶ How wonderful are your gifts to me;
  how good they are!

⁷ I praise the LORD, because he guides
    me,
  and in the night my conscience warns
    me.
⁸ I am always aware of the LORD's
    presence;
  he is near, and nothing can shake me.

⁹ And so I am thankful and glad,
  and I feel completely secure,
¹⁰ because you protect me from the power
    of death.
  I have served you faithfully,
    and you will not abandon me to the
      world of the dead.

¹¹ You will show me the path that leads
    to life;
  your presence fills me with joy
  and brings me pleasure forever.

The Prayer of an Innocent Manʸ

17 Listen, O LORD, to my plea for
      justice;
  pay attention to my cry for help!
  Listen to my honest prayer.
² You will judge in my favor,
  because you know what is right.

³ You know my heart.
  You have come to me at night;
  you have examined me completely
  and found no evil desire in me.
  I speak no evil, ⁴ as others do;
  I have obeyed your command
  and have not followed paths of
    violence.

ʸ HEBREW TITLE: *A prayer by David.*

⁵ I have always walked in your way
   and have never strayed from it.

⁶ I pray to you, O God, because you
      answer me;
   so turn to me and listen to my words.
⁷ Reveal your wonderful love and save
      me;
   at your side I am safe from my
      enemies.

⁸ Protect me as you would your very
      eyes;
   hide me in the shadow of your wings
⁹   from the attacks of the wicked.

   Deadly enemies surround me;
¹⁰   they have no pity and speak proudly.
¹¹ They are around me now, wherever I
      turn,
   watching for a chance to pull me
      down.
¹² They are like lions, waiting for me,
   wanting to tear me to pieces.

¹³ Come, LORD! Oppose my enemies and
      defeat them!
   Save me from the wicked by your
      sword;
¹⁴   save me from those who in this life
      have all they want.
   Punish them with the sufferings you
      have stored up for them;
   may there be enough for their
      children
   and some left over for their children's
      children!

¹⁵ But I will see you, because I have done
      no wrong;
   and when I awake, your presence will
      fill me with joy.

David's Song of Victory [z]

(2 Samuel 22.1-51)

18 How I love you, LORD!
You are my defender.

2 The LORD is my protector;
he is my strong fortress.
My God is my protection,
and with him I am safe.
He protects me like a shield;
he defends me and keeps me safe.
3 I call to the LORD,
and he saves me from my enemies.
Praise the LORD!

4 The danger of death was all around me;
the waves of destruction rolled over
me.
5 The danger of death was around me,
and the grave set its trap for me.
6 In my trouble I called to the LORD;
I called to my God for help.
In his temple he heard my voice;
he listened to my cry for help.

7 Then the earth trembled and shook;
the foundations of the mountains
rocked and quivered,
because God was angry.
8 Smoke poured out of his nostrils,
a consuming flame and burning coals
from his mouth.
9 He tore the sky open and came down
with a dark cloud under his feet.
10 He flew swiftly on his winged creature; [x]
he traveled on the wings of the wind.
11 He covered himself with darkness;
thick clouds, full of water,
surrounded him.

[z] HEBREW TITLE: *The words that David, the LORD's servant, sang to the LORD on the day the LORD saved him from Saul and all his other enemies.* [x] WINGED CREATURES: *See Word List.*

¹² Hailstones and flashes of fire
    came from the lightning before him
    and broke through the dark clouds.

¹³ Then the LORD thundered from the sky;
    and the voice of the Most High was
        heard.ᵃ
¹⁴ He shot his arrows and scattered his
        enemies;
    with flashes of lightning he sent them
        running.
¹⁵ The floor of the ocean was laid bare,
    and the foundations of the earth were
        uncovered,
  when you rebuked your enemies, LORD,
    and roared at them in anger.

¹⁶ The LORD reached down from above
        and took hold of me;
    he pulled me out of the deep waters.
¹⁷ He rescued me from my powerful
        enemies
    and from all those who hate me—
    they were too strong for me.
¹⁸ When I was in trouble, they attacked
        me,
    but the LORD protected me.
¹⁹ He helped me out of danger;
    he saved me because he was pleased
        with me.

²⁰ The LORD rewards me because I do
        what is right;
    he blesses me because I am innocent.
²¹ I have obeyed the law of the LORD;
    I have not turned away from my
        God.
²² I have observed all his laws;
    I have not disobeyed his commands.

ᵃ One ancient translation (and see 2 S 22.14) was heard; Hebrew was
heard hailstones and flashes of fire.

²³ He knows that I am faultless,
    that I have kept myself from doing
      wrong.
²⁴ And so he rewards me because I do
      what is right,
    because he knows that I am innocent.

²⁵ O Lord, you are faithful to those who
      are faithful to you;
    completely good to those who are
      perfect.
²⁶ You are pure to those who are pure,
    but hostile to those who are wicked.
²⁷ You save those who are humble,
    but you humble those who are proud.

²⁸ O Lord, you give me light;
    you dispel my darkness.
²⁹ You give me strength to attack my
      enemies
    and power to overcome their
      defenses.

³⁰ This God—how perfect are his deeds!
    How dependable his words!
  He is like a shield
    for all who seek his protection.
³¹ The Lord alone is God;
    God alone is our defense.
³² He is the God who makes me strong,
    who makes my pathway safe.
³³ He makes me sure-footed as a deer;
    he keeps me safe on the mountains.
³⁴ He trains me for battle,
    so that I can use the strongest bow.

³⁵ O Lord, you protect me and save me;
    your care has made me great,
    and your power has kept me safe.
³⁶ You have kept me from being captured,
    and I have never fallen.
³⁷ I pursue my enemies and catch them;
    I do not stop until I destroy them.

³⁸ I strike them down, and they cannot
   rise;
   they lie defeated before me.
³⁹ You give me strength for the battle
   and victory over my enemies.
⁴⁰ You make my enemies run from me;
   I destroy those who hate me.
⁴¹ They cry for help, but no one saves
   them;
   they call to the LORD, but he does
   not answer.
⁴² I crush them, so that they become like
   dust
   which the wind blows away.
   I trample on them like mud in the
   streets.

⁴³ You saved me from a rebellious people
   and made me ruler over the nations;
   people I did not know have now
   become my subjects.
⁴⁴ Foreigners bow before me;
   when they hear me, they obey.
⁴⁵ They lose their courage
   and come trembling from their
   fortresses.

⁴⁶ The LORD lives! Praise my defender!
   Proclaim the greatness of the God
   who saves me.
⁴⁷ He gives me victory over my enemies;
   he subdues the nations under me
⁴⁸   and saves me from my foes.

   O LORD, you give me victory over my
   enemies
   and protect me from violent men.
⁴⁹ And so I praise you among the nations;
   I sing praises to you.

⁵⁰ God gives great victories to his king;
   he shows constant love to the one he
   has chosen,
   to David and his descendants forever.

God's Glory in Creation[b]

19 How clearly the sky reveals
God's glory!
How plainly it shows what he has
done!
2 Each day announces it to the following
day;
each night repeats it to the next.
3 No speech or words are used,
no sound is heard;
4 yet their message[c] goes out to all the
world
and is heard to the ends of the earth.
God made a home in the sky for the
sun;
5 it comes out in the morning like a
happy bridegroom,
like an athlete eager to run a race.
6 It starts at one end of the sky
and goes across to the other.
Nothing can hide from its heat.

The Law of the LORD

7 The law of the LORD is perfect;
it gives new strength.
The commands of the LORD are
trustworthy,
giving wisdom to those who lack it.
8 The laws of the LORD are right,
and those who obey them are happy.
The commands of the LORD are just
and give understanding to the mind.
9 Reverence for the LORD is good;
it will continue forever.
The judgments of the LORD are just;
they are always fair.
10 They are more desirable than the finest
gold;
they are sweeter than the purest
honey.

[b] HEBREW TITLE: *A psalm by David.* [c] *Some ancient translations*
message; *Hebrew* line.

¹¹ They give knowledge to me, your
servant;
I am rewarded for obeying them.

¹² No one can see his own errors;
deliver me, LORD, from hidden faults!
¹³ Keep me safe, also, from willful sins;
don't let them rule over me.
Then I shall be perfect
and free from the evil of sin.

¹⁴ May my words and my thoughts be
acceptable to you,
O LORD, my refuge and my redeemer!

A Prayer for Victory^d

20 May the LORD answer you when
you are in trouble!
May the God of Jacob protect you!
² May he send you help from his Temple
and give you aid from Mount Zion.
³ May he accept all your offerings
and be pleased with all your
sacrifices.
⁴ May he give you what you desire
and make all your plans succeed.
⁵ Then we will shout for joy over your
victory
and celebrate your triumph by
praising our God.
May the LORD answer all your
requests.

⁶ Now I know that the LORD gives
victory to his chosen king;
he answers him from his holy heaven
and by his power gives him great
victories.

---

^d HEBREW TITLE: *A psalm by David.*

⁷ Some trust in their war chariots
     and others in their horses,
     but we trust in the power of the
     LORD our God.
⁸ Such people will stumble and fall,
     but we will rise and stand firm.

⁹ Give victory to the king, O LORD;
     answerᵉ us when we call.

Praise for Victoryᶠ

21   The king is glad, O LORD,
         because you gave him
         strength;
   he rejoices because you made him
     victorious.
² You have given him his heart's desire;
     you have answered his request.

³ You came to him with great blessings
     and set a crown of gold on his head.
⁴ He asked for life, and you gave it,
     a long and lasting life.

⁵ His glory is great because of your help;
     you have given him fame and
     majesty.
⁶ Your blessings are with him forever,
     and your presence fills him with joy.

⁷ The king trusts in the LORD Almighty;
     and because of the LORD's constant
     love
   he will always be secure.
⁸ The king will capture all his enemies;
     he will capture everyone who hates
     him.
⁹ He will destroy them like a blazing fire
     when he appears.

ᵉ *Some ancient translations* answer; *Hebrew* he will answer.
ᶠ HEBREW TITLE: *A psalm by David.*

The LORD will devour them in his
anger,
and fire will consume them.
10 None of their descendants will survive;
the king will kill them all.

11 They make their plans, and plot against
him,
but they will not succeed.
12 He will shoot his arrows at them
and make them turn and run.

13 We praise you, LORD, for your great
strength!
We will sing and praise your power.

A Cry of Anguish and a Song of Praise*

22 My God, my God, why have you
abandoned me?
I have cried desperately for help,
but still it does not come.
2 During the day I call to you, my God,
but you do not answer;
I call at night,
but get no rest.
3 But you are enthroned as the Holy
One,
the one whom Israel praises.
4 Our ancestors put their trust in you;
they trusted you, and you saved them.
5 They called to you and escaped from
danger;
they trusted you and were not
disappointed.

6 But I am no longer a man; I am a
worm,
despised and scorned by everyone!
7 All who see me make fun of me;
they stick out their tongues and shake
their heads.

* HEBREW TITLE: *A psalm by David.*

8 "You relied on the LORD," they say.
   "Why doesn't he save you?
   If the LORD likes you,
      why doesn't he help you?"

9 It was you who brought me safely
      through birth,
   and when I was a baby, you kept me
      safe.
10 I have relied on you since the day I was
      born,
   and you have always been my God.
11 Do not stay away from me!
   Trouble is near,
   and-there is no one to help.

12 Many enemies surround me like bulls;
   they are all around me,
   like fierce bulls from the land of
      Bashan.
13 They open their mouths like lions,
   roaring and tearing at me.

14 My strength is gone,
   gone like water spilled on the ground.
   All my bones are out of joint;
   my heart is like melted wax.
15 My throat*h* is as dry as dust,
   and my tongue sticks to the roof of
      my mouth.
   You have left me for dead in the dust.

16 A gang of evil men is around me;
   like a pack of dogs they close in on
      me;
   they tear at*i* my hands and feet.
17 All my bones can be seen.
   My enemies look at me and stare.
18 They gamble for my clothes
   and divide them among themselves.

h Probable text throat; *Hebrew* strength.   *i Some ancient translations*
they tear at; *others* they tie; *Hebrew* like a lion.

Come quickly to my rescue! (22.19)

¹⁹ O LORD, don't stay away from me!
    Come quickly to my rescue!
²⁰ Save me from the sword;
    save my life from these dogs.
²¹ Rescue me from these lions;
    I am helpless[j] before these wild bulls.

²² I will tell my people what you have
        done;
    I will praise you in their assembly:
²³ "Praise him, you servants of the LORD!
    Honor him, you descendants of
        Jacob!
    Worship him, you people of Israel!
²⁴ He does not neglect the poor or ignore
        their suffering;
    he does not turn away from them,
    but answers when they call for help."

²⁵ In the full assembly I will praise you
        for what you have done;
    in the presence of those who worship
        you
    I will offer the sacrifices I promised.

[j] *Some ancient translations* I am helpless; *Hebrew* you answered me.

26 The poor will eat as much as they want;
  those who come to the LORD will
    praise him.
May they prosper forever!

27 All nations will remember the LORD.
  From every part of the world they
    will turn to him;
  all races will worship him.
28 The LORD is king,
  and he rules the nations.

29 All proud men will bow down to him;[k]
  all mortal men will bow down before
    him.
30 Future generations will serve him;
  men will speak of the Lord to the
    coming generation.
31 People not yet born will be told:
  "The LORD saved his people."

The LORD Our Shepherd[l]

23 The LORD is my shepherd;
  I have everything I need.
2 He lets me rest in fields of green grass
  and leads me to quiet pools of fresh
    water.
3 He gives me new strength.
  He guides me in the right paths,
    as he has promised.
4 Even if I go through the deepest
    darkness,
  I will not be afraid, LORD,
  for you are with me.
Your shepherd's rod and staff protect
    me.

5 You prepare a banquet for me,
  where all my enemies can see me;

---

[k] *Probable text* will bow down to him; *Hebrew* will eat and bow
down. [l] HEBREW TITLE: *A psalm by David.*

you welcome me as an honored guest
and fill my cup to the brim.
6 I know that your goodness and love
will be with me all my life;
and your house will be my home as
long as I live.

The Great King[m]

24 The world and all that is in it
belong to the LORD;
the earth and all who live on it are
his.
2 He built it on the deep waters beneath
the earth
and laid its foundations in the ocean
depths.

3 Who has the right to go up the LORD's
hill?[n]
Who may enter his holy Temple?
4 Those who are pure in act and in
thought,
who do not worship idols
or make false promises.
5 The LORD will bless them and save
them;
God will declare them innocent.
6 Such are the people who come to God,
who come into the presence of the
God of Jacob.

7 Fling wide the gates,
open the ancient doors,
and the great king will come in.
8 Who is this great king?
He is the LORD, strong and mighty,
the LORD, victorious in battle.

---

[m] HEBREW TITLE: *A psalm by David.*   [n] THE LORD'S HILL: *The hill in Jerusalem on which the Temple was built.*

9 Fling wide the gates,
   open the ancient doors,
   and the great king will come in.
10 Who is this great king?
  The triumphant LORD—he is the great
    king!

A Prayer for Guidance and Protection*

25 To you, O LORD, I offer my
       prayer;
2 in you, my God, I trust.
  Save me from the shame of defeat;
   don't let my enemies gloat over me!
3 Defeat does not come to those who
    trust in you,
  but to those who are quick to rebel
    against you.

4 Teach me your ways, O LORD;
  make them known to me.
5 Teach me to live according to your
    truth,
  for you are my God, who saves me.
  I always trust in you.

6 Remember, O LORD, your kindness and
    constant love
  which you have shown from long
    ago.
7 Forgive the sins and errors of my
    youth.
  In your constant love and goodness,
   remember me, LORD!

8 Because the LORD is righteous and
    good,
  he teaches sinners the path they
    should follow.
9 He leads the humble in the right way
  and teaches them his will.

*HEBREW TITLE: By David.

¹⁰ With faithfulness and love he leads
 all who keep his covenant and obey
 his commands.

¹¹ Keep your promise, LORD, and forgive
 my sins,
 for they are many.
¹² Those who obey the LORD
 will learn from him the path they
 should follow.
¹³ They will always be prosperous,
 and their children will possess the
 land.
¹⁴ The LORD is the friend of those who
 obey him
 and he affirms his covenant with
 them.

¹⁵ I look to the LORD for help at all times,
 and he rescues me from danger.
¹⁶ Turn to me, LORD, and be merciful to
 me,
 because I am lonely and weak.
¹⁷ Relieve me of my worries
 and save me from all my troubles.
¹⁸ Consider my distress and suffering
 and forgive all my sins.

¹⁹ See how many enemies I have;
 see how much they hate me.
²⁰ Protect me and save me;
 keep me from defeat.
 I come to you for safety.
²¹ May my goodness and honesty preserve
 me,
 because I trust in you.

²² From all their troubles, O God,
 save your people Israel!

The Prayer of a Good Man[p]

26 Declare me innocent, O LORD,
because I do what is right
and trust you completely.
2 Examine me and test me, LORD;
judge my desires and thoughts.
3 Your constant love is my guide;
your faithfulness always leads me.[q]

4 I do not keep company with worthless
people;
I have nothing to do with hypocrites.
5 I hate the company of evil men
and avoid the wicked.

6 LORD, I wash my hands to show that I
am innocent
and march in worship around your
altar.
7 I sing a hymn of thanksgiving
and tell of all your wonderful deeds.

8 I love the house where you live, O
LORD,
the place where your glory dwells.
9 Do not destroy me with the sinners;
spare me from the fate of
murderers—
10 men who do evil all the time
and are always ready to take bribes.

11 As for me, I do what is right;
be merciful to me and save me!

12 I am safe from all dangers;
in the assembly of his people I praise
the LORD.

[p] HEBREW TITLE: *By David.* [q] your faithfulness always leads me; *or*
I live in loyalty to you.

A Prayer of Praise[r]

27 The LORD is my light and my
salvation;
I will fear no one.
The LORD protects me from all danger;
I will never be afraid.

2 When evil men attack me and try to kill
me,
they stumble and fall.
3 Even if a whole army surrounds me,
I will not be afraid;
even if enemies attack me,
I will still trust God.[s]

4 I have asked the LORD for one thing;
one thing only do I want:
to live in the LORD's house all my life,
to marvel there at his goodness,
and to ask for his guidance.
5 In times of trouble he will shelter me;
he will keep me safe in his Temple
and make me secure on a high rock.
6 So I will triumph over my enemies
around me.
With shouts of joy I will offer
sacrifices in his Temple;
I will sing, I will praise the LORD.

7 Hear me, LORD, when I call to you!
Be merciful and answer me!
8 When you said, "Come worship me,"
I answered, "I will come, LORD."
9 Don't hide yourself from me!

Don't be angry with me;
don't turn your servant away.
You have been my help;
don't leave me, don't abandon me,
O God, my savior.

[r] HEBREW TITLE: *By David.* [s] still trust God; *or* not lose courage.

10 My father and mother may abandon
     me,
　　but the LORD will take care of me.

11 Teach me, LORD, what you want me to
     do,
　　and lead me along a safe path,
　　because I have many enemies.
12 Don't abandon me to my enemies,
　　who attack me with lies and threats.

13 I know that I will live to see
　　the LORD's goodness in this present
　　　life.
14 Trust in the LORD.
　　Have faith, do not despair.
　　Trust in the LORD.

A Prayer for Help[1]

28 O LORD, my defender, I call to
　　　　you.
　　Listen to my cry!
　If you do not answer me,
　　I will be among those who go down
　　　to the world of the dead.
2 Hear me when I cry to you for help,
　　when I lift my hands toward your
　　　holy Temple.
3 Do not condemn me with the wicked,
　　with those who do evil—
　　men whose words are friendly,
　　but who have hatred in their hearts.

4 Punish them for what they have done,
　　for the evil they have committed.
　Punish them for all their deeds;
　　give them what they deserve!

[1] HEBREW TITLE: *By David.*

5 They take no notice of what the LORD
    has done
  or of what he has made;
 so he will punish them
    and destroy them forever.

6 Give praise to the LORD;
    he has heard my cry for help.
7 The LORD protects and defends me;
    I trust in him.
 He gives me help and makes me glad;
    I praise him with joyful songs.

8 The LORD protects his people;
    he defends and saves his chosen king.
9 Save your people, LORD,
    and bless those who are yours.
 Be their shepherd,
    and take care of them forever.

The Voice of the LORD in the Storm [u]

29 Praise the LORD, you heavenly
        beings;
    praise his glory and power.
2 Praise the LORD's glorious name;
    bow down before the Holy One when
      he appears. [v]

3 The voice of the LORD is heard on the
    seas;
  the glorious God thunders,
    and his voice echoes over the ocean.
4 The voice of the LORD is heard
    in all its might and majesty.

5 The voice of the LORD breaks the
    cedars,
    even the cedars of Lebanon.

---

[u] HEBREW TITLE: *A psalm by David.*   [v] when he appears; *or* in
garments of worship; *or* in his beautiful Temple.

⁶ He makes the mountains of Lebanon
        jump like calves
    and makes Mount Hermon leap like
        a young bull.

⁷ The voice of the LORD makes the
        lightning flash.
⁸ His voice makes the desert shake;
    he shakes the desert of Kadesh.
⁹ The LORD's voice shakes the oaks*ʷ*
    and strips the leaves from the trees
    while everyone in his Temple shouts,
        "Glory to God!"

¹⁰ The LORD rules over the deep waters;
    he rules as king forever.
¹¹ The LORD gives strength to his people
    and blesses them with peace.

A Prayer of Thanksgiving*ˣ*

30   I praise you, LORD, because you
                have saved me
    and kept my enemies from gloating
        over me.
² I cried to you for help, O LORD my
        God,
    and you healed me;
³   you kept me from the grave.
    I was on my way to the depths below,*ʸ*
    but you restored my life.

⁴ Sing praise to the LORD,
    all his faithful people!
Remember what the Holy One has
        done,
    and give him thanks!
⁵ His anger lasts only a moment,
    his goodness for a lifetime.
Tears may flow in the night,
    but joy comes in the morning.

ʷ Probable text shakes the oaks; *Hebrew* makes the deer give birth.
ˣ HEBREW TITLE: *A song for the dedication of the Temple; a psalm by
David. ʸ* THE DEPTHS BELOW: *The world of the dead (see 6.5).*

⁶ I felt secure and said to myself,
  "I will never be defeated."
⁷ You were good to me, LORD;
      you protected me like a mountain
      fortress.
  But then you hid yourself from me,
      and I was afraid.

⁸ I called to you, LORD;
      I begged for your help:
⁹ "What will you gain from my death?
      What profit from my going to the
      grave?
  Are dead people able to praise you?
      Can they proclaim your unfailing
      goodness?
¹⁰ Hear me, LORD, and be merciful!
      Help me, LORD!"

¹¹ You have changed my sadness into a
      joyful dance;
  you have taken away my sorrow
  and surrounded me with joy.
¹² So I will not be silent;
      I will sing praise to you.
  LORD, you are my God;
      I will give you thanks forever.

A Prayer of Trust in God[z]

31 I come to you, LORD, for
      protection;
  never let me be defeated.
  You are a righteous God;
      save me, I pray!
² Hear me! Save me now!
  Be my refuge to protect me;
      my defense to save me.

³ You are my refuge and defense;
      guide me and lead me as you have
      promised.

[z] HEBREW TITLE: *A psalm by David.*

⁴ Keep me safe from the trap that has
        been set for me;
    shelter me from danger.
⁵ I place myself in your care.
    You will save me, LORD;
        you are a faithful God.

⁶ You hate those who worship false gods,
        but I trust in you.
⁷ I will be glad and rejoice
        because of your constant love.
    You see my suffering;
        you know my trouble.
⁸ You have not let my enemies capture
        me;
        you have given me freedom to go
        where I wish.

⁹ Be merciful to me, LORD,
        for I am in trouble;
    my eyes are tired from so much crying;
        I am completely worn out.
¹⁰ I am exhausted by sorrow,
        and weeping has shortened my life.
    I am weak from all my troubles;*
        even my bones are wasting away.

¹¹ All my enemies, and especially my
        neighbors,
        treat me with contempt;
    Those who know me are afraid of me;
        when they see me in the street, they
        run away.
¹² Everyone has forgotten me, as though I
        were dead;
        I am like something thrown away.
¹³ I hear many enemies whispering;
        terror is all around me.
    They are making plans against me,
        plotting to kill me.

a Some ancient translations troubles; *Hebrew* iniquity.

14 But my trust is in you, O LORD;
    you are my God.
15 I am always in your care;
    save me from my enemies,
    from those who persecute me.
16 Look on your servant with kindness;
    save me in your constant love.
17 I call to you, LORD;
    don't let me be disgraced.
  May the wicked be disgraced;
    may they go silently down to the
    world of the dead.
18 Silence those liars—
    all the proud and arrogant
    who speak with contempt about
    righteous men.

19 How wonderful are the good things
    you keep for those who honor you!
  Everyone knows how good you are,
    how securely you protect those who
    trust you.
20 You hide them in the safety of your
    presence
    from the plots of men;
  in a safe shelter you hide them
    from the insults of their enemies.

21 Praise the LORD!
  How wonderfully he showed his love
    for me
    when I was surrounded and attacked!
22 I was afraid and thought
    that he had driven me out of his
    presence.
  But he heard my cry,
    when I called to him for help.

23 Love the LORD, all his faithful people.
  The LORD protects the faithful,
    but punishes the proud as they
    deserve.

²⁴ Be strong, be courageous,
all you that hope in the LORD.

Confession and Forgiveness[b]

32 Happy are those whose sins are
forgiven,
whose wrongs are pardoned.
² Happy is the man whom the LORD does
not accuse of doing wrong
and who is free from all deceit.

³ When I did not confess my sins,
I was worn out from crying all day
long.
⁴ Day and night you punished me, LORD;
my strength was completely drained,
as moisture is dried up by the
summer heat.

⁵ Then I confessed my sins to you;
I did not conceal my wrongdoings.
I decided to confess them to you,
and you forgave all my sins.

⁶ So all your loyal people should pray to
you in times of need;[c]
when a great flood of trouble comes
rushing in,
it will not reach them.
⁷ You are my hiding place;
you will save me from trouble.
I sing aloud of your salvation,
because you protect me.

⁸ The LORD says, "I will teach you the
way you should go;
I will instruct you and advise you.

[b] HEBREW TITLE: *A poem by David.*   [c] *Some ancient translations*
need; *Hebrew* finding only.

⁹ Don't be stupid like a horse or a mule,
    which must be controlled with a bit
      and bridle
    to make it submit."

¹⁰ The wicked will have to suffer,
    but those who trust in the Lord
    are protected by his constant love.
¹¹ You that are righteous, be glad and
      rejoice
    because of what the Lord has done.
You that obey him, shout for joy!

A Song of Praise

33 All you that are righteous,
    shout for joy for what the Lord
      has done;
    praise him, all you that obey him.
² Give thanks to the Lord with harps,
    sing to him with stringed instruments.
³ Sing a new song to him,
    play the harp with skill, and shout for
      joy!

⁴ The words of the Lord are true,
    and all his works are dependable.
⁵ The Lord loves what is righteous and
      just;
    his constant love fills the earth.

⁶ The Lord created the heavens by his
      command,
    the sun, moon, and stars by his
      spoken word.
⁷ He gathered all the seas into one place;
    he shut up the ocean depths in
      storerooms.

⁸ Have reverence for the Lord, all the
      earth!
Honor him, all peoples of the world!

[9] When he spoke, the world was created;
  at his command everything appeared.

[10] The LORD frustrates the purposes of the
    nations;
  he keeps them from carrying out their
    plans.
[11] But his plans endure forever;
  his purposes last eternally.
[12] Happy is the nation whose God is the
    LORD;
  happy are the people he has chosen
    for his own!

[13] The LORD looks down from heaven
  and sees all mankind.
[14] From where he rules, he looks down
  on all who live on earth.
[15] He forms all their thoughts
  and knows everything they do.

[16] A king does not win because of his
    powerful army;
  a soldier does not triumph because of
    his strength.
[17] War horses are useless for victory;
  their great strength cannot save.

[18] The LORD watches over those who have
    reverence for him,
  those who trust in his constant love.
[19] He saves them from death;
  he keeps them alive in times of
    famine.

[20] We put our hope in the LORD;
  he is our protector and our help.
[21] We are glad because of him;
  we trust in his holy name.

[22] May your constant love be with us,
    LORD,
  as we put our hope in you.

In Praise of God's Goodness[d]

34 I will always thank the LORD;
 I will never stop praising him.
[2] I will praise him for what he has done;
 may all who are oppressed listen and
 be glad!
[3] Proclaim with me the LORD's greatness;
 let us praise his name together!

[4] I prayed to the LORD, and he answered
 me;
 he freed me from all my fears.
[5] The oppressed look to him and are
 glad;
 they will never be disappointed.
[6] The helpless call to him, and he
 answers;
 he saves them from all their troubles.
[7] His angel guards those who have
 reverence for the LORD
 and rescues them from danger.

[8] Find out for yourself how good the
 LORD is.
 Happy are those who find safety with
 him.
[9] Have reverence for the LORD, all his
 people;
 those who obey him have all they
 need.
[10] Even lions go hungry for lack of food,
 but those who obey the LORD lack
 nothing good.

[11] Come, my young friends, and listen to
 me,
 and I will teach you to have
 reverence for the LORD.
[12] Would you like to enjoy life?
 Do you want long life and happiness?

[d] HEBREW TITLE: *By David, who left the presence of Abimelech after
pretending to be crazy and being sent away by him.*

¹³ Then keep from speaking evil
    and from telling lies.
¹⁴ Turn away from evil and do good;
    strive for peace with all your heart.

¹⁵ The LORD watches over the righteous
    and listens to their cries;
¹⁶ but he opposes those who do evil,
    so that when they die, they are soon
    forgotten.
¹⁷ The righteous call to the LORD, and he
    listens;
    he rescues them from all their
    troubles.
¹⁸ The LORD is near to those who are
    discouraged;
    he saves those who have lost all
    hope.

¹⁹ The good man suffers many troubles,
    but the LORD saves him from them
    all;
²⁰ the LORD preserves him completely;
    not one of his bones is broken.
²¹ Evil will kill the wicked;
    those who hate the righteous will be
    punished.

²² The LORD will save his people;
    those who go to him for protection
    will be spared.

A Prayer for Help[e]

35 Oppose those who oppose me,
      LORD,
    and fight those who fight against me!
² Take your shield and armor
    and come to my rescue.
³ Lift up your spear and war ax
    against those who pursue me.
Promise that you will save me.

[e] HEBREW TITLE: *By David.*

4 May those who try to kill me
be defeated and disgraced!
May those who plot against me
be turned back and confused!
5 May they be like straw blown by the
wind
as the angel of the LORD pursues
them!
6 May their path be dark and slippery
while the angel of the LORD strikes
them down!

7 Without any reason they laid a trap for
me
and dug a deep hole to catch me.
8 But destruction will catch them before
they know it;
they will be caught in their own trap
and fall to their destruction!

9 Then I will be glad because of the
LORD;
I will be happy because he saved me.
10 With all my heart I will say to the
LORD,
"There is no one like you.
You protect the weak from the
strong,
the poor from the oppressor."

11 Evil men testify against me
and accuse me of crimes I know
nothing about.
12 They pay me back evil for good,
and I sink in despair.
13 But when they were sick, I dressed in
mourning;
I deprived myself of food;
I prayed with my head bowed low,
14   as I would pray for a friend or a
brother.
I went around bent over in mourning,
as one who mourns for his mother.

¹⁵ But when I was in trouble, they were
        all glad
    and gathered around to make fun of
        me;
  strangers beat me
    and kept striking me.
¹⁶ Like men who would mock a cripple,*
    they glared at me with hate.

¹⁷ How much longer, Lord, will you just
        look on?
    Rescue me from their attacks;
    save my life from these lions!
¹⁸ Then I will thank you in the assembly
        of your people;
    I will praise you before them all.

¹⁹ Don't let my enemies, those liars,
    gloat over my defeat.
  Don't let those who hate me for no
        reason
    smirk with delight over my sorrow.

²⁰ They do not speak in a friendly way;
    instead they invent all kinds of lies
        about peace-loving people.
²¹ They accuse me, shouting,
    "We saw what you did!"
²² But you, O LORD, have seen this.
    So don't be silent, Lord;
    don't keep yourself far away!
²³ Rouse yourself, O Lord, and defend me;
    rise up, my God, and plead my cause.
²⁴ You are righteous, O LORD, so declare
        me innocent;
    don't let my enemies gloat over me.
²⁵ Don't let them say to themselves,
    "We are rid of him!
    That's just what we wanted!"

*Like ... cripple; *Hebrew unclear.*

²⁶ May those who gloat over my suffering
    be completely defeated and confused;
may those who claim to be better than I
    am
    be covered with shame and disgrace.

²⁷ May those who want to see me
    acquitted
    shout for joy and say again and again,
"How great is the LORD!
    He is pleased with the success of his
    servant."
²⁸ Then I will proclaim your
    righteousness,
    and I will praise you all day long.

The Wickedness of Man[s]

36 Sin speaks to the wicked man
    deep in his heart;
he rejects God and does not have
    reverence for him.
² Because he thinks so highly of himself,
    he thinks that God will not discover
    his sin and condemn it.
³ His speech is wicked and full of lies;
    he no longer does what is wise and
    good.
⁴ He makes evil plans as he lies in bed;
    nothing he does is good,
    and he never rejects anything evil.

The Goodness of God

⁵ LORD, your constant love reaches the
    heavens;
    your faithfulness extends to the skies.
⁶ Your righteousness is towering like the
    mountains;
    your justice is like the depths of the
    sea.
    Men and animals are in your care.

[s] HEBREW TITLE: *By David, the LORD's servant.*

⁷ How precious, O God, is your constant
    love!
    We find˟ protection under the
      shadow of your wings.
⁸ We feast on the abundant food you
    provide;
    you let us drink from the river of
      your goodness.
⁹ You are the source of all life,
    and because of your light we see the
      light.

¹⁰ Continue to love those who know you
    and to do good to those who are
      righteous.
¹¹ Do not let proud men attack me
    or wicked men make me run away.

¹² See where evil men have fallen.
    There they lie, unable to rise.

The Destiny of the Wicked and of the Goodʰ

37 Don't be worried on account of
      the wicked;
    don't be jealous of those who do
      wrong.
² They will soon disappear like grass that
    dries up;
    they will die like plants that wither.

³ Trust in the LORD and do good;
    live in the land and be safe.
⁴ Seek your happiness in the LORD,
    and he will give you your heart's
      desire.

⁵ Give yourself to the LORD;
    trust in him, and he will help you;
⁶ he will make your righteousness shine
    like the noonday sun.

˟ precious, O God, is . . . find; *or* precious is your constant love!
Gods and men find. ʰ HEBREW TITLE: *By David.*

7 Be patient and wait for the LORD to act;
    don't be worried about those who
        prosper
    or those who succeed in their evil
        plans.

8 Don't give in to worry or anger;
    it only leads to trouble.
9 Those who trust in the LORD will
        possess the land,
    but the wicked will be driven out.

10 Soon the wicked will disappear;
    you may look for them, but you
        won't find them;
11 but the humble will possess the land
    and enjoy prosperity and peace.

12 The wicked man plots against the good
        man
    and glares at him with hate.
13 But the Lord laughs at wicked men,
    because he knows they will soon be
        destroyed.

14 The wicked draw their swords and bend
        their bows
    to kill the poor and needy,
    to slaughter those who do what is
        right;
15 but they will be killed by their own
        swords,
    and their bows will be smashed.

16 The little that a good man owns
    is worth more than the wealth of all
        the wicked,
17 because the LORD will take away the
        strength of the wicked,
    but protect those who are good.

18 The LORD takes care of those who obey
    him,
  and the land will be theirs forever.
19 They will not suffer when times are
    bad;
  they will have enough in time of
    famine.
20 But the wicked will die;
  the enemies of the LORD will vanish
    like wild flowers;
  they will disappear like smoke.

21 The wicked man borrows and never
    pays back,
  but the good man is generous with
    his gifts.
22 Those who are blessed by the LORD
    will possess the land,
  but those who are cursed by him will
    be driven out.

23 The LORD guides a man in the way he
    should go
  and protects those who please him.
24 If they fall, they will not stay down,
  because the LORD will help them up.

25 I am an old man now; I have lived a
    long time,
  but I have never seen a good man
    abandoned by the LORD
  or his children begging for food.
26 At all times he gives freely and lends to
    others,
  and his children are a blessing.

27 Turn away from evil and do good,
  and your descendants will always live
    in the land;
28 for the LORD loves what is right
  and does not abandon his faithful
    people.

He protects them forever,
    but the descendants of the wicked
      will be driven out.
29 The righteous will possess the land
    and live in it forever.

30 A good man's words are wise,
    and he is always fair.
31 He keeps the law of his God in his
      heart
    and never departs from it.

32 A wicked man watches a good man
    and tries to kill him;
33 but the LORD will not abandon him to
      his enemy's power
    or let him be condemned when he is
      on trial.

34 Put your hope in the LORD and obey
      his commands;
    he will honor you by giving you the
      land,
    and you will see the wicked driven
      out.

35 I once knew a wicked man who was a
      tyrant;
    he towered over everyone like a
      cedar of Lebanon;[i]
36 but later I[j] passed by, and he wasn't
      there;
    I looked for him, but couldn't find
      him.

37 Notice the good man, observe the
      righteous man;
    a peaceful man has descendants,
38 but sinners are completely destroyed,
    and their descendants are wiped out.

[i] *One ancient translation* like a cedar of Lebanon; *Hebrew unclear.*
[j] *Some ancient translations* I; *Hebrew* he.

³⁹ The LORD saves righteous men
  and protects them in times of trouble.
⁴⁰ He helps them and rescues them;
  he saves them from the wicked,
  because they go to him for protection.

The Prayer of a Suffering Man *ᵏ*

38 O LORD, don't punish me in your
     anger!
² You have wounded me with your
  arrows;
  you have struck me down.

³ Because of your anger, I am in great
  pain;
  my whole body is diseased because of
  my sins.
⁴ I am drowning in the flood of my sins;
  they are a burden too heavy to bear.

⁵ Because I have been foolish,
  my sores stink and rot.
⁶ I am bent over, I am crushed;
  I mourn all day long.
⁷ I am burning with fever
  and I am near death.
⁸ I am worn out and utterly crushed;
  my heart is troubled, and I groan
  with pain.

⁹ O Lord, you know what I long for;
  you hear all my groans.
¹⁰ My heart is pounding, my strength is
  gone,
  and my eyes have lost their
  brightness.
¹¹ My friends and neighbors will not come
  near me,
  because of my sores;
  even my family keeps away from me.

ᵏ HEBREW TITLE: *A psalm by David; a lament.*

¹² Those who want to kill me lay traps for
me,
and those who want to hurt me
threaten to ruin me;
they never stop plotting against me.

¹³ I am like a deaf man and cannot hear,
like a dumb man and cannot speak.
¹⁴ I am like a man who does not answer,
because he cannot hear.

¹⁵ But I trust in you, O LORD;
and you, O Lord my God, will
answer me.
¹⁶ Don't let my enemies gloat over my
distress;
don't let them boast about my
downfall!
¹⁷ I am about to fall
and am in constant pain.

¹⁸ I confess my sins;
they fill me with anxiety.
¹⁹ My enemies are healthy and strong;
there are many who hate me for no
reason.
²⁰ Those who pay back evil for good
are against me because I try to do
right.

²¹ Do not abandon me, O LORD;
do not stay away, my God!
²² Help me now, O Lord my savior!

The Confession of a Suffering Man[1]

39 I said, "I will be careful about
what I do
and will not let my tongue make me
sin;
I will not say anything
while evil men are near."

[1] HEBREW TITLE: *A psalm by David.*

² I kept quiet, not saying a word,
        not even about anything good!
But my suffering only grew worse,
³   and I was overcome with anxiety.
The more I thought, the more troubled
        I became;
    I could not keep from asking:
⁴ "LORD, how long will I live?
        When will I die?
    Tell me how soon my life will end."

⁵ How short you have made my life!
        In your sight my lifetime seems
        nothing.
    Indeed every living man is no more
        than a puff of wind,
⁶   no more than a shadow.
All he does is for nothing;
        he gathers wealth, but doesn't know
        who will get it.

⁷ What, then, can I hope for, Lord?
        I put my hope in you.
⁸ Save me from all my sins,
        and don't let fools make fun of me.
⁹ I will keep quiet, I will not say a word,
        for you are the one who made me
        suffer like this.
¹⁰ Don't punish me any more!
        I am about to die from your blows.
¹¹ You punish a man's sins by your
        rebukes,
    and like a moth you destroy what he
        loves.
    Indeed a man is no more than a puff of
        wind!

¹² Hear my prayer, LORD,
        and listen to my cry;
        come to my aid when I weep.
    Like all my ancestors
        I am only your guest for a little
        while.

¹³ Leave me alone so that I may have
    some happiness
before I go away and am no more.

A Song of Praise [m]

40 I waited patiently for the LORD's
        help;
    then he listened to me and heard my
        cry.
² He pulled me out of a dangerous pit,
    out of the deadly quicksand.
He set me safely on a rock
    and made me secure.
³ He taught me to sing a new song,
    a song of praise to our God.
Many who see this will take warning
    and will put their trust in the LORD.

⁴ Happy are those who trust the LORD,
    who do not turn to idols
    or join those who worship false gods.
⁵ You have done many things for us, O
        LORD our God;
    there is no one like you!
    You have made many wonderful
        plans for us.
I could never speak of them all—
    their number is so great!

⁶ You do not want sacrifices and
        offerings;
    you do not ask for animals burned
        whole on the altar
    or for sacrifices to take away sins.
Instead, you have given me ears to hear
        you,
⁷ and so I answered, "Here I am;
    your instructions for me are in the
        book of the Law." [n]

---

[m] HEBREW TITLE: *A psalm by David.*   [n] your instructions . . . Law;
or my devotion to you is recorded in your book.

⁸ How I love to do your will, my God!
I keep your teaching in my heart."

⁹ In the assembly of all your people,
LORD,
I told the good news that you save us.
You know that I will never stop
telling it.
¹⁰ I have not kept the news of salvation to
myself;
I have always spoken of your
faithfulness and help.
In the assembly of all your people I
have not been silent
about your loyalty and constant love.

¹¹ LORD, I know you will never stop being
merciful to me.
Your love and loyalty will always
keep me safe.

A Prayer for Help
(Psalm 70)

¹² I am surrounded by many troubles—
too many to count!
My sins have caught up with me,
and I can no longer see;
they are more than the hairs of my
head,
and I have lost my courage.
¹³ Save me, LORD! Help me now!
¹⁴ May those who try to kill me
be completely defeated and confused.
May those who are happy because of
my troubles
be turned back and disgraced.
¹⁵ May those who make fun of me
be dismayed by their defeat.

¹⁶ May all who come to you
be glad and joyful.

May all who are thankful for your
  salvation
    always say, "How great is the LORD!"

17 I am weak and poor, O Lord,
    but you have not forgotten me.
  You are my savior and my God—
    hurry to my aid!

The Prayer of a Sick Man[o]

41 Happy are those who are
    concerned for the poor;
  the LORD will help them when they
    are in trouble.
2 The LORD will protect them and
    preserve their lives;
  he will make them happy in the land;
  he will not abandon them to the
    power of their enemies.
3 The LORD will help them when they
    are sick
  and will restore them to health.

4 I said, "I have sinned against you,
    LORD;
  be merciful to me and heal me."
5 My enemies say cruel things about me.
  They want me to die and be
    forgotten.
6 Those who come to see me are not
    sincere;
  they gather bad news about me
  and then go out and tell it
    everywhere.
7 All who hate me whisper to each other
    about me,
  they imagine the worst about[p] me.
8 They say, "He is fatally ill;
  he will never leave his bed again."

---

[o] HEBREW TITLE: *A psalm by David.* [p] imagine the worst about: *or*
make evil plans to harm.

9 Even my best friend, the one I trusted
        most,
    the one who shared my food,
    has turned against me.

10 Be merciful to me, LORD, and restore
        my health,
    and I will pay my enemies back.
11 They will not triumph over me,
    and I will know that you are pleased
        with me.
12 You will help me, because I do what is
        right;
    you will keep me in your presence
        forever.

13 Praise the LORD, the God of Israel!
    Praise him now and forever!

Amen! Amen!

BOOK TWO
(Psalms 42—72)

The Prayer of a Man in Exile *q*

42 As a deer longs for a stream of
        cool water,
    so I long for you, O God.
2 I thirst for you, the living God.
    When can I go and worship in your
        presence?
3 Day and night I cry,
    and tears are my only food;
    all the time my enemies ask me,
    "Where is your God?"

q HEBREW TITLE: *A poem by the clan of Korah.*

4 My heart breaks when I remember the
    past,
    when I went with the crowds to the
    house of God
    and led them as they walked along,
    a happy crowd, singing and shouting
    praise to God.
5 Why am I so sad?
    Why am I so troubled?
I will put my hope in God,
    and once again I will praise him,
    my savior and my God.

6-7 Here in exile my heart is breaking,
    and so I turn my thoughts to him.
He has sent waves of sorrow over my
    soul;
    chaos roars at me like a flood,
    like waterfalls thundering down to
    the Jordan
    from Mount Hermon and Mount
    Mizar.
8 May the LORD show his constant love
    during the day,
    so that I may have a song at night,
    a prayer to the God of my life.

9 To God, my defender, I say,
    "Why have you forgotten me?
Why must I go on suffering
    from the cruelty of my enemies?"
10 I am crushed by their insults,
    as they keep on asking me,
    "Where is your God?"

11 Why am I so sad?
    Why am I so troubled?
I will put my hope in God,
    and once again I will praise him,
    my savior and my God.

The Prayer of a Man in Exile
(Continuation of Psalm 42)

43 O God, declare me innocent,
and defend my cause against
the ungodly;
deliver me from lying and evil men!
2 You are my protector;
why have you abandoned me?
Why must I go on suffering
from the cruelty of my enemies?

3 Send your light and your truth;
may they lead me
and bring me back to Zion, your
sacred hill,'
and to your Temple, where you live.
4 Then I will go to your altar, O God;
you are the source of my happiness.
I will play my harp and sing praise to
you,
O God, my God.

5 Why am I so sad?
Why am I so troubled?
I will put my hope in God,
and once again I will praise him,
my savior and my God.

A Prayer for Protection*

44 With our own ears we have heard
it, O God—
our ancestors have told us about it,
about the great things you did in their
time,
in the days of long ago:
2 how you yourself drove out the heathen
and established your people in their
land;
how you punished the other nations
and caused your own to prosper.

' SACRED HILL: *See 2.6.*   * HEBREW TITLE: *A poem by the clan of Korah.*

3 Your people did not conquer the land
   with their swords;
   they did not win it by their own
      power;
  it was by your power and your strength,
   by the assurance of your presence,
   which showed that you loved them.

4 You are my king and my God;
   you give[1] victory to your people,
5   and by your power we defeat our
      enemies.
6 I do not trust in my bow
   or in my sword to save me;
7 but you have saved us from our
      enemies
   and defeated those who hate us.
8 We will always praise you
   and give thanks to you forever.

9 But now you have rejected us and let us
      be defeated;
   you no longer march out with our
      armies.
10 You made us run from our enemies,
   and they took for themselves what
      was ours.
11 You allowed us to be slaughtered like
      sheep;
   you scattered us in foreign countries.
12 You sold your own people for a small
      price
   as though they had little value.[u]

13 Our neighbors see what you did to us,
   and they mock us and laugh at us.
14 You have made us a joke among the
      nations;
   they shake their heads at us in scorn.

[1] Some ancient translations and my God; you give; Hebrew O God;
give. [u] as . . . value; or and made no profit from the sale.

¹⁵ I am always in disgrace;
　　I am covered with shame
¹⁶　　from hearing the sneers and insults
　　　of my enemies and those who hate
　　　me.

¹⁷ All this has happened to us,
　　. even though we have not forgotten
　　　　you
　　　or broken the covenant you made
　　　　with us.
¹⁸ We have not been disloyal to you;
　　we have not disobeyed your
　　　　commands.
¹⁹ Yet you left us helpless among wild
　　　animals;
　　you abandoned us in deepest
　　　darkness.

²⁰ If we had stopped worshiping our God
　　and prayed to a foreign god,
²¹ you would surely have discovered it,
　　because you know our secret
　　　thoughts.
²² But it is on your account that we are
　　　being killed all the time,
　　that we are treated like sheep to be
　　　slaughtered.

²³ Wake up, Lord! Why are you asleep?
　　Rouse yourself! Don't reject us
　　　forever!
²⁴ Why are you hiding from us?
　　Don't forget our suffering and
　　　trouble!

²⁵ We fall crushed to the ground;
　　we lie defeated in the dust.
²⁶ Come to our aid!
　　Because of your constant love save
　　　us!

A Royal Wedding Song [v]

45 Beautiful words fill my mind,
as I compose this song for the
king.
Like the pen of a good writer
my tongue is ready with a poem.

2 You are the most handsome of men;
you are an eloquent speaker.
God has always blessed you.
3 Buckle on your sword, mighty king;
you are glorious and majestic.

4 Ride on in majesty to victory
for the defense of truth and justice! [w]
Your strength will win you great
victories!
5 Your arrows are sharp,
they pierce the hearts of your
enemies;
nations fall down at your feet.

6 The kingdom that God has given you [x]
will last forever and ever.
You rule over your people with justice;
7 you love what is right and hate what
is evil.
That is why God, your God, has chosen
you
and has poured out more happiness
on you
than on any other king.
8 The perfume of myrrh and aloes is on
your clothes;
musicians entertain you in palaces
decorated with ivory.

[v] HEBREW TITLE: *A poem by the clan of Korah; a love song.*
[w] *Probable text* and justice; *Hebrew* and meekness of justice.   [x] The
kingdom that God has given you; *or* Your kingdom, O God; *or*
Your divine kingdom.

⁹ Among the ladies of your court are
      daughters of kings,
   and at the right of your throne stands
      the queen,
   wearing ornaments of finest gold.

¹⁰ Bride of the king, listen to what I say—
      forget your people and your relatives.
¹¹ Your beauty will make the king desire
      you;
   he is your master, so you must obey
      him.
¹² The people of Tyre will bring you gifts;
   rich people will try to win your favor.

¹³ The princess is in the palace—how
      beautiful she is!
   Her gown is made of gold thread.
¹⁴ In her colorful gown she is led to the
      king,
   followed by her bridesmaids,
   and they also are brought to him.
¹⁵ With joy and gladness they come
   and enter the king's palace.

¹⁶ You, my king, will have many sons
      to succeed your ancestors as kings,
   and you will make them rulers over
      the whole earth.
¹⁷ My song will keep your fame alive
      forever,
   and everyone will praise you for all
      time to come.

God Is with Us ʸ

46   God is our shelter and strength,
         always ready to help in times of
         trouble.

ʸ HEBREW TITLE: *A song by the clan of Korah.*

We will not be afraid. (46.2)

2 So we will not be afraid, even if the
   earth is shaken
      and mountains fall into the ocean
      depths;
3 even if the seas roar and rage,
      and the hills are shaken by the
      violence.

4 There is a river that brings joy to the
   city of God,
      to the sacred house of the Most High.
5 God is in that city, and it will never be
   destroyed;
      at early dawn he will come to its aid.
6 Nations are terrified, kingdoms are
   shaken;
      God thunders, and the earth
      dissolves.

7 The LORD Almighty is with us;
      the God of Jacob is our refuge.

⁸ Come and see what the LORD has done.
   See what amazing things he has done
      on earth.
⁹ He stops wars all over the world;
   he breaks bows, destroys spears,
      and sets shields on fire.
¹⁰ "Stop fighting," he says, "and know that
      I am God,
   supreme among the nations,
   supreme over the world."

¹¹ The LORD Almighty is with us;
   the God of Jacob is our refuge.

Sing praise to God. (47.6)

The Supreme Ruler²

47 Clap your hands for joy, all
      peoples!
   Praise God with loud songs!
² The LORD, the Most High, is to be
      feared;
   he is a great king, ruling over all the
      world.

² HEBREW TITLE: *A psalm by the clan of Korah.*

3 He gave us victory over the peoples;
    he made us rule over the nations.
4 He chose for us the land where we live,
    the proud possession of his people,
      whom he loves.

5 God goes up to his throne.
    There are shouts of joy and the blast
      of trumpets,
    as the LORD goes up.
6 Sing praise to God;
    sing praise to our king!
7 God is king over all the world;
    praise him with songs!

8 God sits on his sacred throne;
    he rules over the nations.
9 The rulers of the nations assemble
    with the people*a* of the God of
      Abraham.
  More powerful than all armies is he;
    he rules supreme.

Zion, the City of God*b*

48   The LORD is great and is to be
        highly praised
    in the city of our God, on his sacred
      hill.*c*
2 Zion, the mountain of God, is high and
      beautiful;
    the city of the great king brings joy to
      all the world.
3 God has shown that there is safety with
      him
    inside the fortresses of the city.

4 The kings gathered together
    and came to attack Mount Zion.

---

a Probable text with the people; *Hebrew* the people.   *b* HEBREW
TITLE: *A psalm by the clan of Korah; a song.*   *c* SACRED HILL: *See*
2.6.

5 But when they saw it, they were
        amazed;
    they were afraid and ran away.
6 There they were seized with fear and
        anguish,
    like a woman about to bear a child,
7   like ships tossing in a furious storm.

8 We have heard what God has done,
    and now we have seen it
    in the city of our God, the LORD
        Almighty;
    he will keep the city safe forever.

9 Inside your Temple, O God,
    we think of your constant love.
10 You are praised by people everywhere,
    and your fame extends over all the
        earth.
    You rule with justice;
11   let the people of Zion be glad!
    You give right judgments;
    let there be joy in the cities of Judah!

12 People of God, walk around Zion and
        count the towers;
13   take notice of the walls and examine
        the fortresses,
    so that you may tell the next
        generation:
14   "This God is our God forever and
        ever;
    he will lead us for all time to come."

The Foolishness of Trusting in Riches[d]

49 Hear this, everyone!
    Listen, all people everywhere,
2   great and small alike,
    rich and poor together.

[d] HEBREW TITLE: *A psalm by the clan of Korah.*

³ My thoughts will be clear;
   I will speak words of wisdom.
⁴ I will turn my attention to proverbs
   and explain their meaning as I play
      the harp.

⁵ I am not afraid in times of danger
   when I am surrounded by enemies,
⁶ by evil men who trust in their riches
   and boast of their great wealth.
⁷ A person can never redeem himself;
   he cannot pay God the price for his
      life,
⁸   because the payment for a human life
      is too great.
   What he could pay would never be
      enough
⁹   to keep him from the grave,
      to let him live forever.

¹⁰ Anyone can see that even wise men die,
   as well as foolish and stupid men.
   They all leave their riches to their
      descendants.
¹¹ Their gravesᵉ are their homes forever;
   there they stay for all time,
   though they once had lands of their
      own.
¹² A man's greatness cannot keep him
      from death;
   he will still die like the animals.

¹³ See what happens to those who trust in
      themselves,
   the fate of thoseᶠ who are satisfied
      with their wealth—
¹⁴ they are doomed to die like sheep,
   and Death will be their shepherd.

ᵉ *Some ancient translations* graves; *Hebrew* inner thoughts. ᶠ *One*
ancient translation the fate of those; *Hebrew* after them.

The righteous will triumph over them,
as their bodies quickly decay
in the world of the dead far from
their homes.[g]
15 But God will rescue me;
he will save me from the power of
death.

16 Don't be upset when a man becomes
rich,
when his wealth grows even greater;
17 he cannot take it with him when he
dies;
his wealth will not go with him to the
grave.
18 Even if a man is satisfied with this life
and is praised because he is
successful,
19 he will join all his ancestors in death,
where the darkness lasts forever.
20 A man's greatness cannot keep him
from death;
he will still die like the animals.

True Worship[h]

50 The Almighty God, the LORD,
speaks;
he calls to the whole earth from east
to west.
2 God shines from Zion,
the city perfect in its beauty.

3 Our God is coming, but not in silence;
a raging fire is in front of him,
a furious storm around him.
4 He calls heaven and earth as witnesses
to see him judge his people.

[g] in . . . homes.; *Hebrew unclear.*   [h] HEBREW TITLE: *A psalm by
Asaph.*

5 He says, "Gather my faithful people to
　　me,
　　those who made a covenant with me
　　　by offering a sacrifice."
6 The heavens proclaim that God is
　　righteous,
　　that he himself is judge.

7 "Listen, my people, and I will speak;
　　I will testify against you, Israel.
　　I am God, your God.
8 I do not reprimand you because of your
　　sacrifices
　　and the burnt offerings you always
　　　bring me.
9 And yet I do not need bulls from your
　　farms
　　or goats from your flocks;
10 all the animals in the forest are mine
　　and the cattle on thousands of hills.
11 All the wild birds are mine
　　and all living things in the fields.

12 "If I were hungry, I would not ask you
　　for food,
　　for the world and everything in it is
　　　mine.
13 Do I eat the flesh of bulls
　　or drink the blood of goats?
14 Let the giving of thanks be your
　　sacrifice to God,*i*
　　and give the Almighty all that you
　　　promised.
15 Call to me when trouble comes;
　　I will save you,
　　and you will praise me."

16 But God says to the wicked,
　　"Why should you recite my
　　　commandments?
　　Why should you talk about my
　　　covenant?

i Let the giving . . . to God; or Offer your thanksgiving sacrifice to
God.

The animals in the forest are mine. (50.10)

17 You refuse to let me correct you;
     you reject my commands.
18 You become the friend of every thief
     you see,
       and you associate with adulterers.

19 "You are always ready to speak evil;
     you never hesitate to tell lies.
20 You are ready to accuse your own
     brothers
       and to find fault with them.
21 You have done all this, and I have said
     nothing,
       so you thought that I am like you.
   But now I reprimand you
     and make the matter plain to you.

22 "Listen to this, you that ignore me,
     or I will destroy you,
       and there will be no one to save you.
23 Giving thanks is the sacrifice that
     honors me,
       and I will surely save all who obey
       me."

A Prayer for Forgiveness[j]

51 Be merciful to me, O God,
     because of your constant love.
   Because of your great mercy
     wipe away my sins!
2 Wash away all my evil
     and make me clean from my sin!

3 I recognize my faults;
     I am always conscious of my sins.
4 I have sinned against you—only against
     you—
       and done what you consider evil.
   So you are right in judging me;
     you are justified in condemning me.

---

[j] HEBREW TITLE: *A psalm by David, after the prophet Nathan had spoken to him about his adultery with Bathsheba.*

⁵ I have been evil from the day I was
    born;
    from the time I was conceived, I have
    been sinful.

⁶ Sincerity and truth are what you
    require;
    fill my mind with your wisdom.
⁷ Remove my sin, and I will be clean;
    wash me, and I will be whiter than
    snow.
⁸ Let me hear the sounds of joy and
    gladness;
    and though you have crushed me and
    broken me,
    I will be happy once again.
⁹ Close your eyes to my sins
    and wipe out all my evil.

¹⁰ Create a pure heart in me, O God,
    and put a new and loyal spirit in me.
¹¹ Do not banish me from your presence;
    do not take your holy spirit away
    from me.
¹² Give me again the joy that comes from
    your salvation,
    and make me willing to obey you.
¹³ Then I will teach sinners your
    commands,
    and they will turn back to you.

¹⁴ Spare my life, O God, and save me,ᵏ
    and I will gladly proclaim your
    righteousness.
¹⁵ Help me to speak, Lord,
    and I will praise you.

¹⁶ You do not want sacrifices,
    or I would offer them;
    you are not pleased with burnt
    offerings.

ᵏ Spare my life . . . me; *or* O God my savior, keep me from the
crime of murder.

17 My sacrifice is a humble spirit, O God;
    you will not reject a humble and
        repentant heart.

18 O God, be kind to Zion and help her;
    rebuild the walls of Jerusalem.
19 Then you will be pleased with proper
        sacrifices
    and with our burnt offerings;
    and bulls will be sacrificed on your
        altar.

God's Judgment and Grace[1]

52 Why do you boast, great man, of
        your evil?
    God's faithfulness is eternal.
2 You make plans to ruin others;
    your tongue is like a sharp razor.
    You are always inventing lies.
3 You love evil more than good
    and falsehood more than truth.
4 You love to hurt people with your
        words, you liar!

5 So God will ruin you forever;
    he will take hold of you and snatch
        you from your home;
    he will remove you from the world of
        the living.
6 Righteous people will see this and be
        afraid;
    Then they will laugh at you and say,
7 "Look, here is a man who did not
        depend on God for safety,
    but trusted instead in his great wealth
    and looked for security in being
        wicked."

[1] HEBREW TITLE: *A poem by David, after Doeg the Edomite went to Saul and told him that David had gone to the house of Ahimelech.*

8 But I am like an olive tree growing in
     the house of God;
  I trust in his constant love forever
     and ever.
9 I will always thank you, God, for what
     you have done;
  in the presence of your people
  I will proclaim that you are good.

The Wickedness of Men[m]

(Psalm 14)

53 Fools say to themselves,
       "There is no God."
  They are all corrupt,
     and they have done terrible things;
     there is no one who does what is
        right.

2 God looks down from heaven at
     mankind
  to see if there are any who are wise,
  any who worship him.
3 But they have all turned away;
     they are all equally bad.
  Not one of them does what is right,
     not a single one.

4 "Don't they know?" God asks.
     "Are these evildoers ignorant?
  They live by robbing my people,
     and they never pray to me."

5 But then they will become terrified,
     as they have never been before,
     for God will scatter the bones of the
        enemies of his people.
  God has rejected them,
     and so Israel will totally defeat them.

[m] HEBREW TITLE: *A poem by David.*

6 How I pray that victory
  will come to Israel from Zion.
How happy the people of Israel will be
  when God makes them prosperous
    again!

A Prayer for Protection from Enemies[n]

54 Save me by your power, O God;
    set me free by your might!
2 Hear my prayer, O God;
  listen to my words!
3 Proud men are coming to attack me;
  cruel men are trying to kill me—
  men who do not care about God.

4 But God is my helper.
  The Lord is my defender.
5 May God use their own evil to punish
    my enemies.
  He will destroy them because he is
    faithful.

6 I will gladly offer you a sacrifice, O
    LORD;
  I will give you thanks
  because you are good.
7 You have rescued me from all my
    troubles,
  and I have seen my enemies defeated.

The Prayer of a Man Betrayed by a Friend[o]

55 Hear my prayer, O God;
    don't turn away from my plea!
2 Listen to me and answer me;
  I am worn out by my worries.

[n] HEBREW TITLE: *A poem by David, after the men from Ziph went to Saul and told him that David was hiding in their territory.*   [o] HEBREW TITLE: *A poem by David.*

I wish I had wings like a dove. (55.6)

³ I am terrified by the threats of my
  enemies,
 crushed by the oppression of the
  wicked.
They bring trouble on me;
 they are angry with me and hate me.

⁴ I am terrified,
 and the terrors of death crush me.
⁵ I am gripped by fear and trembling;
 I am overcome with horror.
⁶ I wish I had wings like a dove.
 I would fly away and find rest.
⁷ I would fly far away
 and live in the wilderness.
⁸ I would hurry and find myself a shelter
 from the raging wind and the storm.
⁹ Confuse the speech of my enemies, O
  Lord!

 I see violence and riots in the city,
¹⁰ surrounding it day and night,
  filling it with crime and trouble.

11 There is destruction everywhere;
    the streets are full of oppression and
       fraud.

12 If it were an enemy making fun of me,
    I could endure it;
  if it were an opponent boasting over
      me,
    I could hide myself from him.
13 But it is you, my companion,
    my colleague and close friend.
14 We had intimate talks with each other
    and worshiped together in the
      Temple.
15 May my enemies die before their time;
    may they go down alive into the
      world of the dead!
  Evil is in their homes and in their
      hearts.

16 But I call to the LORD God for help,
    and he will save me.
17 Morning, noon, and night
    my complaints and groans go up to
      him,
    and he will hear my voice.
18 He will bring me safely back
    from the battles that I fight
    against so many enemies.
19 God, who has ruled from eternity,
    will hear me and defeat them;
  for they refuse to change,
    and they do not fear him.

20 My former companion attacked his
      friends;
  he broke his promises.
21 His words were smoother than cream,
    but there was hatred in his heart;
  his words were as soothing as oil,
    but they cut like sharp swords.

22 Leave your troubles with the LORD,
   and he will defend you;
   he never lets honest men be defeated.

23 But you, O God, will bring those
        murderers and liars to their graves
   before half their life is over.
   As for me, I will trust in you.

A Prayer of Trust in God[p]

56 Be merciful to me, O God,
      because I am under attack;
   my enemies persecute me all the
      time.
2 All day long my opponents attack me.
   There are so many who fight against
      me.
3 When I am afraid, O LORD Almighty,
   I put my trust in you.
4 I trust in God and am not afraid;
   I praise him for what he has
      promised.
   What can a mere human being do to
      me?

5 My enemies make trouble for me all
      day long;
   they are always thinking up some
      way to hurt me!
6 They gather in hiding places
   and watch everything I do,
   hoping to kill me.
7 Punish[q] them, O God, for their evil;
   defeat those people in your anger!

8 You know how troubled I am;
   you have kept a record of my tears.
   Aren't they listed in your book?

[p] HEBREW TITLE: *A psalm by David, after the Philistines captured him in Gath.*   [q] *Probable text* Punish; *Hebrew* Save.

⁹ The day I call to you,
  my enemies will be turned back.
I know this: God[r] is on my side—
¹⁰   the LORD, whose promises I praise.
¹¹ In him I trust, and I will not be afraid.
   What can a mere human being do to
     me?

¹² O God, I will offer you what I have
     promised;
   I will give you my offering of
     thanksgiving,
¹³ because you have rescued me from
     death
   and kept me from defeat.
And so I walk in the presence of God,
  in the light that shines on the living.

A Prayer for Help[s]

57 Be merciful to me, O God, be
      merciful,
   because I come to you for safety.
In the shadow of your wings I find
     protection
  until the raging storms are over.

² I call to God, the Most High,
  to God, who supplies my every need.
³ He will answer from heaven and save
     me;
  he will defeat my oppressors.
  God will show me his constant love
    and faithfulness.

⁴ I am surrounded by enemies,
  who are like man-eating lions.
Their teeth are like spears and arrows;
  their tongues are like sharp swords.

[r] I know this: God; *or* Because I know that God.   [s] HEBREW TITLE:
A psalm by David, after he fled from Saul in the cave.

⁵ Show your greatness in the sky, O God,
    and your glory over all the earth.

⁶ My enemies have spread a net to catch
      me;
    I am overcome with distress.
  They dug a pit in my path,
    but fell into it themselves.

⁷ I have complete confidence, O God;
    I will sing and praise you!
⁸ Wake up, my soul!
    Wake up, my harp and lyre!
    I will wake up the sun.
⁹ I will thank you, O Lord, among the
      nations.
    I will praise you among the peoples.
¹⁰ Your constant love reaches the heavens;
    your faithfulness touches the skies.
¹¹ Show your greatness in the sky, O God,
    and your glory over all the earth.

A Prayer for God to Punish the Wicked[i]

58 Do you rulers[u] ever give a just
           decision?
      Do you judge all men fairly?
² No! You think only of the evil you can
      do,
    and commit crimes of violence in the
      land.

³ Evil men go wrong all their lives;
    they tell lies from the day they are
      born.
⁴ They are full of poison like snakes;
    they stop up their ears like a deaf
      cobra,
⁵ which does not hear the voice of the
      snake charmer,
    or the chant of the clever magician.

[i] HEBREW TITLE: *A psalm by David.*   [u] rulers; *or* gods.

⁶ Break the teeth of these fierce lions, O
God.
⁷ May they disappear like water draining
away;
may they be crushed like weeds on a
path.ᵛ
⁸ May they be like snails that dissolve
into slime;
may they be like a baby born dead
that never sees the light.
⁹ Before they know it, they are cut down
like weeds;
in his fierce anger God will blow
them away
while they are still living.ʷ

¹⁰ The righteous will be glad when they
see sinners punished;
they will wade through the blood of
the wicked.
¹¹ People will say, "The righteous are
indeed rewarded;
there is indeed a God who judges the
world."

A Prayer for Safetyˣ

59 Save me from my enemies, my
God;
protect me from those who attack me!
² Save me from those evil men;
rescue me from those murderers!

³ Look! They are waiting to kill me;
cruel men are gathering against me.
It is not because of any sin or wrong I
have done,
⁴ nor because of any fault of mine, O
LORD,
that they hurry to their places.

ᵛ *Probable text* may ... path; *Hebrew unclear.* ʷ *Verse 9 in Hebrew
is unclear.* ˣ HEBREW TITLE: *A psalm by David, after Saul sent men
to watch his house in order to kill him.*

⁵ Rise, LORD God Almighty, and come to
     my aid;
  see for yourself, God of Israel!
Wake up and punish the heathen;
  show no mercy to evil traitors!

⁶ They come back in the evening,
    snarling like dogs as they go about
      the city.
⁷ Listen to their insults and threats.
  Their tongues are like swords in their
      mouths,
    yet they think that no one hears
      them.

⁸ But you laugh at them, LORD;
    you mock all the heathen.
⁹ I have confidence in your strength;
    you are my refuge, O God.
¹⁰ My God loves me and will come to me;
    he will let me see my enemies
      defeated.

¹¹ Do not kill them, O God, or my people
     may forget.
  Scatter them by your strength and
      defeat them,
  O Lord, our protector.
¹² Sin is on their lips; all their words are
      sinful;
    may they be caught in their pride!
  Because they curse and lie,
¹³   destroy them in your anger;
    destroy them completely.
  Then everyone will know that God
      rules in Israel,
    that his rule extends over all the
      earth.

¹⁴ My enemies come back in the evening,
    snarling like dogs as they go about
      the city,

15   like dogs roaming about for food
and growling if they do not find
enough.

16 But I will sing about your strength;
every morning I will sing aloud of
your constant love.
You have been a refuge for me,
a shelter in my time of trouble.
17 I will praise you, my defender.
My refuge is God,
the God who loves me.

A Prayer for Deliverance[y]

60 You have rejected us, God, and
defeated us;
you have been angry with us—but
now turn back to us.[z]
2 You have made the land tremble, and
you have cut it open;
now heal its wounds, because it is
falling apart.
3 You have made your people suffer
greatly;
we stagger around as though we were
drunk.
4 You have warned those who have
reverence for you,
so that they might escape
destruction.
5 Save us by your might; answer our
prayer,
so that the people you love may be
rescued.

[y] HEBREW TITLE: *A psalm by David, for teaching, when he fought against the Arameans from Naharaim and from Zobah, and Joab turned back and killed 12,000 Edomites in Salt Valley.*   [z] angry with us . . us; *or* angry with us and turned your back on us.

⁶ From his sanctuary*ᵃ* God has said,
    "In triumph I will divide Shechem
    and distribute Sukkoth Valley to my
        people.
⁷ Gilead is mine, and Manasseh too;
    Ephraim is my helmet
    and Judah my royal scepter.
⁸ But I will use Moab as my washbowl,
    and I will throw my sandals on
        Edom,
    as a sign that I own it.
Did the Philistines think they would
    shout in triumph over me?"

⁹ Who, O God, will take me into the
    fortified city?
    Who will lead me to Edom?
¹⁰ Have you really rejected us?
    Aren't you going to march out with
        our armies?
¹¹ Help us against the enemy;
    human help is worthless.
¹² With God on our side we will win;
    he will defeat our enemies.

A Prayer for Protection*ᵇ*

61   Hear my cry, O God;
      listen to my prayer!
² In despair and far from home
    I call to you!

Take me to a safe refuge,
³   for you are my protector,
    my strong defense against my
        enemies.

⁴ Let me live in your sanctuary all my
    life;
    let me find safety under your wings.

ᵃ From his sanctuary; *or* In his holiness.   *ᵇ* HEBREW TITLE: *By David.*

Take me to a safe refuge. (61.2)

⁵ You have heard my promises, O God,
and you have given me what belongs
to those who honor you.

⁶ Add many years to the king's life;
let him live on and on!
⁷ May he rule forever in your presence,
O God;
protect him with your constant love
and faithfulness.

⁸ So I will always sing praises to you,
as I offer you daily what I have
promised.

Confidence in God's Protection*c*

62 I wait patiently for God to save
me;
I depend on him alone.

c HEBREW TITLE: *A psalm by David.*

2 He alone protects and saves me;
  he is my defender,
  and I shall never be defeated.

3 How much longer will all of you attack
    a man
  who is no stronger than a broken-
    down fence?
4 You only want to bring him down from
    his place of honor;
  you take pleasure in lies.
 You speak words of blessing,
  but in your heart you curse him.

5 I depend on God alone;
  I put my hope in him.
6 He alone protects and saves me;
  he is my defender,
  and I shall never be defeated.
7 My salvation and honor depend on
    God;
  he is my strong protector;
  he is my shelter.

8 Trust in God at all times, my people.
  Tell him all your troubles,
  for he is our refuge.

9 Men are all like a puff of breath;
  great and small alike are worthless.
 Put them on the scales, and they weigh
    nothing;
  they are lighter than a mere breath.
10 Don't put your trust in violence;
  don't hope to gain anything by
    robbery;
 even if your riches increase,
  don't depend on them.

11 More than once I have heard God say
    that power belongs to him
12   and that his love is constant.
  You yourself, O Lord, reward everyone
    according to his deeds.

Longing for God[d]

<big>63</big> O God, you are my God,
 and I long for you.
My whole being desires you;
 like a dry, worn-out, and waterless
 land,
 my soul is thirsty for you.
2 Let me see you in the sanctuary;
 let me see how mighty and glorious
 you are.
3 Your constant love is better than life
 itself,
 and so I will praise you.
4 I will give you thanks as long as I live;
 I will raise my hands to you in
 prayer.
5 My soul will feast and be satisfied,
 and I will sing glad songs of praise to
 you.

6 As I lie in bed, I remember you;
 all night long I think of you,
7 because you have always been my
 help.
In the shadow of your wings I sing for
 joy.
8 I cling to you,
 and your hand keeps me safe.

9 Those who are trying to kill me
 will go down into the world of the
 dead.
10 They will be killed in battle,
 and their bodies eaten by wolves.
11 Because God gives him victory,
 the king will rejoice.
Those who make promises in God's
 name will praise him,
 but the mouths of liars will be shut.

[d] HEBREW TITLE: *A psalm by David, when he was in the desert of
Judea.*

A Prayer for Protection[e]

64 I am in trouble, God—listen to
my prayer!
I am afraid of my enemies—save my
life!

2 Protect me from the plots of the
wicked,
from mobs of evil men.
3 They sharpen their tongues like swords
and aim cruel words like arrows.
4 They are quick to spread their
shameless lies;
they destroy good men with cowardly
slander.
5 They encourage each other in their evil
plots;
they talk about where they will place
their traps.
"No one can see them," they say.
6 They make evil plans and say,
"We have planned a perfect crime."
The heart and mind of man are a
mystery.

7 But God shoots his arrows at them,
and suddenly they are wounded.
8 He will destroy them because of those
words;[f]
all who see them will shake their
heads.
9 They will all be afraid;
they will think about what God has
done
and tell about his deeds.
10 All righteous people will rejoice
because of what the LORD has done.
They will find safety in him;
all good people will praise him.

---

[e] HEBREW TITLE: *A psalm by David.*   [f] *Probable text* He will destroy
them because of those words; *Hebrew* They will destroy him, those
words are against them.

Praise and Thanksgiving[g]

65 O God, it is right for us to praise
    you in Zion
and keep our promises to you,
2 because you answer prayers.
People everywhere will come to you
3 on account of their sins.
Our faults defeat us,[h]
    but you forgive them.
4 Happy are those whom you choose,
    whom you bring to live in your
        sanctuary.
We shall be satisfied with the good
        things of your house,
    the blessings of your sacred Temple.

5 You answer us by giving us victory,
    and you do wonderful things to save
        us.
People all over the world
    and across the distant seas trust in
        you.
6 You set the mountains in place by your
        strength,
    showing your mighty power.
7 You calm the roar of the seas
    and the noise of the waves;
    you calm the uproar of the peoples.
8 The whole world stands in awe
    of the great things that you have
        done.
Your deeds bring shouts of joy
    from one end of the earth to the
        other.

9 You show your care for the land by
        sending rain;
    you make it rich and fertile.

[g] HEBREW TITLE: *A psalm by David; a song.*   [h] *One ancient
translation* us; *Hebrew* me.

You fill the streams with water;
   you provide the earth with crops.
This is how you do it:
10   you send abundant rain on the
         plowed fields
   and soak them with water;
   you soften the soil with showers
   and cause the young plants to grow.
11 What a rich harvest your goodness
      provides!
   Wherever you go there is plenty.
12 The pastures are filled with flocks;
   the hillsides are full of joy.
13 The fields are covered with sheep;
   the valleys are full of wheat.
Everything shouts and sings for joy.

A Song of Praise and Thanksgiving[i]

66   Praise God with shouts of joy, all
         people!
2 Sing to the glory of his name;
   offer him glorious praise!
3 Say to God, "How wonderful are the
      things you do!
   Your power is so great
   that your enemies bow down in fear
      before you.
4 Everyone on earth worships you;
   they sing praises to you,
   they sing praises to your name."

5 Come and see what God has done,
   his wonderful acts among men.
6 He changed the sea into dry land;
   our ancestors crossed the river on
      foot.
There we rejoiced because of what he
      did.
7 He rules forever by his might
   and keeps his eyes on the nations.
   Let no rebels rise against him.

[i] HEBREW TITLE: A song.

Sing to the glory of his name. (66.2)

8 Praise our God, all nations;
   let your praise be heard.
9 He has kept us alive
   and has not allowed us to fall.

10 You have put us to the test, God;
    as silver is purified by fire,
    so you have tested us.
11 You let us fall into a trap
    and placed heavy burdens on our
       backs.
12 You let our enemies trample us;
    we went through fire and flood,
    but now you have brought us to a
       place of safety.*j*

13 I will bring burnt offerings to your
       house;
    I will offer you what I promised.
14 I will give you what I said I would
    when I was in trouble.
15 I will offer sheep to be burned on the
       altar;
   I will sacrifice bulls and goats,
      and the smoke will go up to the sky.

16 Come and listen, all who honor God,
    and I will tell you what he has done
       for me.

j Some ancient translations safety: *Hebrew* overflowing.

¹⁷ I cried to him for help;
    I praised him with songs.
¹⁸ If I had ignored my sins,
    the Lord would not have listened to
      me.
¹⁹ But God has indeed heard me;
    he has listened to my prayer.

²⁰ I praise God,
    because he did not reject my prayer
    or keep back his constant love from
      me.

A Song of Thanksgiving[k]

67 God, be merciful to us and bless
      us;
    look on us with kindness,
² so that the whole world may know your
      will;
    so that all nations may know your
      salvation.

³ May the peoples praise you, O God;
    may all the peoples praise you!

⁴ May the nations be glad and sing for
      joy,
    because you judge the peoples with
      justice
    and guide every nation on earth.

⁵ May the peoples praise you, O God;
    may all the peoples praise you!

⁶ The land has produced its harvest;
    God, our God, has blessed us.
⁷ God has blessed us;
    may all people everywhere honor
      him.

[k] HEBREW TITLE: *A psalm; a song.*

A National Song of Triumph[l]

68 God rises up and scatters his
enemies.
Those who hate him run away in
defeat.
2 As smoke is blown away, so he drives
them off;
as wax melts in front of the fire,
so do the wicked perish in God's
presence.
3 But the righteous are glad and rejoice
in his presence;
they are happy and shout for joy.

4 Sing to God, sing praises to his name;
prepare a way for him who rides on
the clouds.[m]
His name is the LORD—be glad in his
presence!

5 God, who lives in his sacred Temple,
cares for orphans and protects
widows.
6 He gives the lonely a home to live in
and leads prisoners out into happy
freedom,
but rebels will have to live in a
desolate land.

7 O God, when you led your people,
when you marched across the desert,
8 the earth shook, and the sky poured
down rain,
because of the coming of the God of
Sinai,[n]
the coming of the God of Israel.
9 You caused abundant rain to fall
and restored your worn-out land;

[l] HEBREW TITLE: *A psalm by David; a song.*   [m] on the clouds; *or*
across the desert.   [n] GOD OF SINAI: *As the people of Israel went from
Egypt to Canaan, God revealed himself to them at Mount Sinai (see
Ex 19.16-25).*

¹⁰ your people made their home there;
 in your goodness you provided for
  the poor.

¹¹ The Lord gave the command,
 and many women carried the news:
¹² "Kings and their armies are running
  away!"
 The women at home divided what
  was captured:
¹³ figures of doves covered with silver,
 whose wings glittered with fine gold.
(Why did some of you stay among the
  sheep pens on the day of battle?)
¹⁴ When Almighty God scattered the
  kings on Mount Zalmon,
 he caused snow to fall there.

¹⁵ What a mighty mountain is Bashan,
 a mountain of many peaks!
¹⁶ Why from your mighty peaks do you
  look with scorn
 on the mountain^o on which God
  chose to live?
 The LORD will live there forever!

¹⁷ With his many thousands of mighty
  chariots
 the Lord comes from Sinai^p into the
  holy place.
¹⁸ He goes up to the heights,
 taking many captives with him;
 he receives gifts from rebellious men.
 The LORD God will live there.

¹⁹ Praise the Lord,
 who carries our burdens day after
  day;
 he is the God who saves us.

^o MOUNTAIN: *See 2.6.*   ^p *Probable text* comes from Sinai; *Hebrew* in
them, Sinai.

20 Our God is a God who saves;
    he is the LORD, our Lord,
    who rescues us from death.

21 God will surely break the heads of his
        enemies,
    of those who persist in their sinful
        ways.
22 The Lord has said, "I will bring your
        enemies back from Bashan;
    I will bring them back from the
        depths of the ocean,
23 so that you may wade in their blood,
    and your dogs may lap up as much as
        they want."

24 O God, your march of triumph is seen
        by all,
    the procession of God, my king, into
        his sanctuary.
25 The singers are in front, the musicians
        are behind,
    in between are the girls beating the
        tambourines.
26 "Praise God in the meeting of his
        people;
    praise the LORD, all you descendants
        of Jacob!"
27 First comes Benjamin, the smallest
        tribe,
    then the leaders of Judah with their
        group,
    followed by the leaders of Zebulun
        and Naphtali.

28 Show your power, O God,
    the power you have used on our
        behalf
29   from your Temple in Jerusalem,
    where kings bring gifts to you.

30 Rebuke Egypt, that wild animal in the
　　　reeds;
　　　rebuke the nations, that herd of bulls
　　　　with their calves,
　　　until they all bow down and offer you
　　　　their silver.
　　Scatter those people who love to make
　　　　war!*q*
31 Ambassadors* will come from Egypt;
　　　the Sudanese will raise their hands in
　　　　prayer to God.

32 Sing to God, kingdoms of the world,
　　　sing praise to the Lord,
33 　to him who rides in the sky,
　　　the ancient sky.
　　Listen to him shout with a mighty roar.
34 Proclaim God's power;
　　　his majesty is over Israel,
　　　his might is in the skies.
35 How awesome is God as he comes from
　　　his sanctuary—
　　　the God of Israel!
　　He gives strength and power to his
　　　people.

　　Praise God!

A Cry for Help*s*

69　Save me, O God!
　　　The water is up to my neck;
2 I am sinking in deep mud,
　　　and there is no solid ground;
　　I am out in deep water,
　　　and the waves are about to drown
　　　　me.
3 I am worn out from calling for help,
　　　and my throat is aching.
　　I have strained my eyes,
　　　looking for your help.

---

q Verse 30 in Hebrew is unclear.　r Some ancient translations
Ambassadors; *Hebrew unclear.　s* HEBREW TITLE: *By David.*

⁴ Those who hate me for no reason
    are more numerous than the hairs of
      my head.
My enemies tell lies against me;
    they are strong and want to kill me.
They made me give back things I did
    not steal.
⁵ My sins, O God, are not hidden from
    you;
    you know how foolish I have been.
⁶ Don't let me bring shame on those who
    trust in you,
    Sovereign LORD Almighty!
Don't let me bring disgrace to those
    who worship you,
    O God of Israel!
⁷ It is for your sake that I have been
    insulted
    and that I am covered with shame.
⁸ I am like a stranger to my brothers,
    like a foreigner to my family.

⁹ My devotion to your Temple burns in
    me like a fire;
    the insults which are hurled at you
    fall on me.
¹⁰ I humble myself‹ by fasting,
    and people insult me;
¹¹ I dress myself in clothes of mourning,
    and they laugh at me.
¹² They talk about me in the streets,
    and drunkards make up songs about
    me.

¹³ But as for me, I will pray to you, LORD;
    answer me, God, at a time you
    choose.
Answer me because of your great love,
    because you keep your promise to
    save.

‹ *Some ancient translations* humble myself; *Hebrew* cry.

14 Save me from sinking in the mud;
keep me safe from my enemies,
safe from the deep water.
15 Don't let the flood come over me;
don't let me drown in the depths
or sink into the grave.

16 Answer me, LORD, in the goodness of
your constant love;
in your great compassion turn to me!
17 Don't hide yourself from your servant;
I am in great trouble—answer me
now!
18 Come to me and save me;
rescue me from my enemies.

19 You know how I am insulted,
how I am disgraced and dishonored;
you see all my enemies.
20 Insults have broken my heart,
and I am in despair.
I had hoped for sympathy, but there
was none;
for comfort, but I found none.
21 When I was hungry, they gave me
poison;
when I was thirsty, they offered me
vinegar.

22 May their banquets cause their ruin;
may their sacred feasts cause their
downfall.
23 Strike them with blindness!
Make their backs always weak!
24 Pour out your anger on them;
let your indignation overtake them.
25 May their camps be left deserted;
may no one be left alive in their
tents.
26 They persecute those whom you have
punished;
they talk about the sufferings of those
you have wounded.

²⁷ Keep a record of all their sins;
> don't let them have any part in your
> salvation.
²⁸ May their names be erased from the
> book of the living;
> may they not be included in the list
> of your people.

²⁹ But I am in pain and despair;
> lift me up, O God, and save me!

³⁰ I will praise God with a song;
> I will proclaim his greatness by
> giving him thanks.
³¹ This will please the LORD more than
> offering him cattle,
> more than sacrificing a full-grown
> bull.
³² When the oppressed see this, they will
> be glad;
> those who worship God will be
> encouraged.
³³ The LORD listens to those in need
> and does not forget his people in
> prison.

³⁴ Praise God, O heaven and earth,
> seas and all creatures in them.
³⁵ He will save Jerusalem
> and rebuild the towns of Judah.
> His people will live there and possess
> the land;
³⁶   the descendants of his servants will
> inherit it,
> and those who love him will live
> there.

A Prayer for Help ᵘ
(Psalm 40.13–17)

70   Save me, O God!
> LORD, help me now!

ᵘ HEBREW TITLE: *A psalm by David; a lament.*

² May those who try to kill me
   be defeated and confused.
May those who are happy because of
      my troubles
   be turned back and disgraced.
³ May those who make fun of me
   be dismayed by their defeat.

⁴ May all who come to you
   be glad and joyful.
May all who are thankful for your
      salvation
   always say, "How great is God!"

⁵ I am weak and poor;
   come to me quickly, O God.
You are my savior and my LORD—
   hurry to my aid!

An Old Man's Prayer

71 LORD, I have come to you for
         protection;
   never let me be defeated!
² Because you are righteous, help me and
      rescue me.
   Listen to me and save me!
³ Be my secure shelter
   and a strong fortress^v to protect me;
   you are my refuge and defense.

⁴ My God, rescue me from wicked men,
   from the power of cruel and evil men.
⁵ Sovereign LORD, I put my hope in you;
   I have trusted in you since I was
      young.
⁶ I have relied on you all my life;
   you have protected^w me since the day
      I was born.
   I will always praise you.

---

^v *One ancient translation* a strong fortress; *Hebrew* to go always you
commanded.   ^w *Some ancient translations* protected; *Hebrew*
unclear.

7 My life has been an example to many,
   because you have been my strong
   defender.
8 All day long I praise you
   and proclaim your glory.
9 Do not reject me now that I am old;
   do not abandon me now that I am
   feeble.
10 My enemies want to kill me;
   they talk and plot against me.
11 They say, "God has abandoned him;
   let's go after him and catch him;
   there is no one to rescue him."

I am old and my hair is gray. (71.18)

¹² Don't stay so far away, O God;
   my God, hurry to my aid!
¹³ May those who attack me
      be defeated and destroyed.
   May those who try to hurt me
      be shamed and disgraced.
¹⁴ I will always put my hope in you;
   I will praise you more and more.
¹⁵ I will tell of your goodness;
      all day long I will speak of your
         salvation,
      though it is more than I can
         understand.
¹⁶ I will praise your power, Sovereign
      LORD;
      I will proclaim your goodness, yours
         alone.

¹⁷ You have taught me ever since I was
         young,
      and I still tell of your wonderful acts.
¹⁸ Now that I am old and my hair is gray,
      do not abandon me, O God!
   Be with me while I proclaim your
         power and might
      to all generations to come.

¹⁹ Your righteousness, God, reaches the
         skies.
      You have done great things;
      there is no one like you.
²⁰ You have sent troubles and suffering on
         me,
      but you will restore my strength;
      you will keep me from the grave.
²¹ You will make me greater than ever;
      you will comfort me again.

²² I will indeed praise you with the harp;
      I will praise your faithfulness, my
         God.
   On my harp I will play hymns to you,
      the Holy One of Israel.

23 I will shout for joy as I play for you;
    with my whole being I will sing
    because you have saved me.
74 I will speak of your righteousness all
    day long,
    because those who tried to harm me
    have been defeated and disgraced.

A Prayer for the King [x]

72 Teach the king to judge with your
    righteousness, O God;
    share with him your own justice,
2 so that he will rule over your people
    with justice
    and govern the oppressed with
    righteousness.
3 May the land enjoy prosperity;
    may it experience righteousness.
4 May the king judge the poor fairly;
    may he help the needy
    and defeat their oppressors.
5 May your people worship you as long
    as the sun shines,
    as long as the moon gives light, for
    ages to come.

6 May the king be like rain on the fields,
    like showers falling on the land.
7 May righteousness flourish in his
    lifetime,
    and may prosperity last as long as the
    moon gives light.

8 His kingdom will reach from sea to sea,
    from the Euphrates to the ends of the
    earth.
9 The peoples of the desert will bow
    down before him;
    his enemies will throw themselves to
    the ground.

[x] HEBREW TITLE: *By Solomon.*

10 The kings of Spain and of the islands
        will offer him gifts;
    the kings of Arabia and Ethiopia will
        bring him offerings.
11 All kings will bow down before him;
    all nations will serve him.

12 He rescues the poor who call to him,
        and those who are needy and
        neglected.
13 He has pity on the weak and poor;
    he saves the lives of those in need.
14 He rescues them from oppression and
        violence;
    their lives are precious to him.

15 Long live the king!
    May he be given gold from Arabia;
    may prayers be said for him at all
        times;
    may God's blessings be on him
        always!
16 May there be plenty of grain in the
        land;
    may the hills be covered with crops,
    as fruitful as those of Lebanon.
    May the cities be filled with people,
    like fields full of grass.
17 May the king's name never be
        forgotten;
    may his fame last as long as the sun.
    May all nations ask God to bless them
    as he has blessed the king. *

18 Praise the LORD, the God of Israel!
    He alone does these wonderful things.
19 Praise his glorious name forever!
    May his glory fill the whole world.

                    Amen! Amen!

* as he has blessed the king; *or* and may they wish happiness for
the king.

²⁰ This is the end of the prayers of David
son of Jesse.

BOOK THREE
(Psalms 73—89)

The Justice of Godʸ

73 God is indeed good to Israel,
      to those who have pure hearts.
² But I had nearly lost confidence;
      my faith was almost gone
³ because I was jealous of the proud
      when I saw that things go well for the
      wicked.

⁴ They do not suffer pain;
      they are strong and healthy.
⁵ They do not suffer as other people do;
      they do not have the troubles that
      others have.
⁶ And so they wear pride like a necklace
      and violence like a robe;
⁷ their hearts pour out evil,ᶻ
      and their minds are busy with wicked
      schemes.
⁸ They laugh at other people and speak
      of evil things;
      they are proud and make plans to
      oppress others.
⁹ They speak evil of God in heaven
      and give arrogant orders to men on
      earth,
¹⁰ so that even God's people turn to them
      and eagerly believe whatever they
      say.ᵃ
¹¹ They say, "God will not know;
      the Most High will not find out."
¹² That is what the wicked are like.
      They have plenty and are always
      getting more.

ʸ HEBREW TITLE: *By Asaph.*   ᶻ *Some ancient translations* their hearts
pour out evil; *Hebrew unclear.*   ᵃ *Verse 10 in Hebrew is unclear.*

¹³ Is it for nothing, then, that I have kept
          myself pure
     and have not committed sin?
¹⁴ O God, you have made me suffer all
          day long;
     every morning you have punished
          me.

¹⁵ If I had said such things,
     I would not be acting as one of your
          people.
¹⁶ I tried to think this problem through,
     but it was too difficult for me
¹⁷   until I went into your Temple.
   Then I understood what will happen to
          the wicked.

¹⁸ You will put them in slippery places
     and make them fall to destruction!
¹⁹ They are instantly destroyed;
     they go down to a horrible end.
²⁰ They are like a dream that goes away in
          the morning;
     when you rouse yourself, O Lord,
          they disappear.

²¹ When my thoughts were bitter
     and my feelings were hurt,
²² I was as stupid as an animal;
     I did not understand you.
²³ Yet I always stay close to you,
     and you hold me by the hand.
²⁴ You guide me with your instruction
     and at the end you will receive me
          with honor.
²⁵ What else do I have in heaven but you?
     Since I have you, what else could I
          want on earth?
²⁶ My mind and my body may grow weak,
     but God is my strength;
     he is all I ever need.

²⁷ Those who abandon you will certainly
    perish;
  you will destroy those who are
    unfaithful to you.
²⁸ But as for me, how wonderful to be
    near God,
  to find protection with the Lord GOD
  and to proclaim all that he has done!

A Prayer for National Deliverance [b]

74 Why have you abandoned us like
      this, O God?
  Will you be angry with your own
    people forever?
² Remember your people, whom you
    chose for yourself long ago,
  whom you brought out of slavery to
    be your own tribe.
  Remember Mount Zion, where once
    you lived.
³ Walk over these total ruins;
  our enemies have destroyed
    everything in the Temple.

⁴ Your enemies have shouted in triumph
    in your Temple;
  they have placed their flags there as
    signs of victory.
⁵ They looked like woodsmen
  cutting down trees with their axes. [c]
⁶ They smashed all the wooden panels
  with their axes and sledge hammers.
⁷ They wrecked your Temple and set it
    on fire;
  they desecrated the place where you
    are worshiped.
⁸ They wanted to crush us completely;
  they burned down every holy place in
    the land.

[b] HEBREW TITLE: *A poem by Asaph.*   [c] *Verse 5 in Hebrew is unclear.*

⁹ All our sacred symbols are gone;
    there are no prophets left,
    and no one knows how long this will
      last.
¹⁰ How long, O God, will our enemies
    laugh at you?
    Will they insult your name forever?
¹¹ Why have you refused to help us?
    Why do you keep your hands behind
    you?ᵈ

¹² But you have been our king from the
    beginning, O God;
    you have saved us many times.
¹³ With your mighty strength you divided
    the sea
    and smashed the heads of the sea
    monsters;
¹⁴ you crushed the heads of the monster
    Leviathanᵉ
    and fed his body to desert animals.ᶠ
¹⁵ You made springs and fountains flow;
    you dried up large rivers.
¹⁶ You created the day and the night;
    you set the sun and the moon in their
    places;
¹⁷ you set the limits of the earth;
    you made summer and winter.

¹⁸ But remember, O Lord, that your
    enemies laugh at you,
    that they are godless and despise you.
¹⁹ Don't abandon your helpless people to
    their cruel enemies;
    don't forget your persecuted people!

²⁰ Remember the covenant you made with
    us.
    There is violence in every dark
    corner of the land.

ᵈ *Probable text* Why do you keep your hands behind you; *Hebrew unclear.*   ᵉ LEVIATHAN: *A legendary monster which was a symbol of the forces of chaos and evil.*   ᶠ animals; *or* people.

21 Don't let the oppressed be put to
        shame;
    let those poor and needy people
        praise you.

22 Rouse yourself, God, and defend your
        cause!
    Remember that godless people laugh
        at you all day long.
23 Don't forget the angry shouts of your
        enemies,
    the continuous noise made by your
        foes.

God the Judge[g]

75 We give thanks to you, O God,
        we give thanks to you!
    We proclaim how great you are
    and tell of[h] the wonderful things you
        have done.

2 "I have set a time for judgment," says
        God,
    "and I will judge with fairness.
3 Though every living creature tremble
    and the earth itself be shaken,
    I will keep its foundations firm.
4 I tell the wicked not to be arrogant;
5   I tell them to stop their boasting."

6 Judgment does not come from the east
        or from the west,
    from the north or from the south;[i]
7 it is God who is the judge,
    condemning some and acquitting
        others.

---

[g] HEBREW TITLE: *A psalm by Asaph; a song.*   [h] *Some ancient
translations* We proclaim how great you are and tell of; *Hebrew*
Your name is near and they tell of.   [i] *Probable text* from the north
or from the south; *Hebrew* from the wilderness of the mountains.

⁸ The LORD holds a cup in his hand,
   filled with the strong wine of his
      anger.
He pours it out, and all the wicked
      drink it;
   they drink it down to the last drop.

⁹ But I will never stop speaking of the
      God of Jacob
   or singing praises to him.
¹⁰ He will break the power of the wicked,
   but the power of the righteous will be
      increased.

God the Victor[j]

76 God is known in Judah;
      his name is honored in Israel.
² He has his home in Jerusalem;
   he lives on Mount Zion.
³ There he broke the arrows of the
      enemy,
   their shields and swords, yes, all their
      weapons.

⁴ How glorious you are, O God!
   How majestic, as you return from the
      mountains
   where you defeated your foes.
⁵ Their brave soldiers have been stripped
      of all they had
   and now are sleeping the sleep of
      death;
   all their strength and skill was
      useless.
⁶ When you threatened them, O God of
      Jacob,
   the horses and their riders fell dead.

⁷ But you, LORD, are feared by all.
   No one can stand in your presence
   when you are angry.

[j] HEBREW TITLE: *A psalm by Asaph; a song.*

⁸ You made your judgment known from
      heaven;
    the world was afraid and kept silent,
⁹ when you rose up to pronounce
      judgment,
    to save all the oppressed on earth.

¹⁰ Men's anger only results in more praise
      for you;
    those who survive the wars will keep
      your festivals.ᵏ

¹¹ Give the LORD your God what you
      promised him;
    bring gifts to him, all you nearby
      nations.
  God makes men fear him;
¹²   he humbles proud princes
    and terrifies great kings.

Comfort in Time of Distressˡ

77   I cry aloud to God;
          I cry aloud, and he hears me.
² In times of trouble I pray to the Lord;
    all night long I lift my hands in
      prayer,
    but I cannot find comfort.
³ When I think of God, I sigh;
    when I meditate, I feel discouraged.

⁴ He keeps me awake all night;
    I am so worried that I cannot speak.
⁵ I think of days gone by
    and remember years of long ago.
⁶ I spend the night in deep thought;ᵐ
    I meditate, and this is what I ask
      myself:

ᵏ One ancient translation will keep your festivals; verse 10 in Hebrew
is unclear. ˡ HEBREW TITLE: A psalm by Asaph. ᵐ Some ancient
translations deep thought; Hebrew song.

7 "Will the Lord always reject us?
   Will he never again be pleased with
      us?
8 Has he stopped loving us?
   Does his promise no longer stand?
9 Has God forgotten to be merciful?
   Has anger taken the place of his
      compassion?"
10 Then I said, "What hurts me most is
      this—
   that God is no longer powerful."[n]

11 I will remember your great deeds,
      LORD;
   I will recall the wonders you did in
      the past.
12 I will think about all that you have
      done;
   I will meditate on all your mighty
      acts.

13 Everything you do, O God, is holy.
   No god is as great as you.
14 You are the God who works miracles;
   you showed your might among the
      nations.
15 By your power you saved your people,
   the descendants of Jacob and of
      Joseph.

16 When the waters saw you, O God, they
      were afraid,
   and the depths of the sea trembled.
17 The clouds poured down rain;
   thunder crashed from the sky,
   and lightning flashed in all directions.
18 The crash of your thunder rolled out,
   and flashes of lightning lit up the
      world;
   the earth trembled and shook.

[n] *Verse 10 in Hebrew is unclear.*

¹⁹ You walked through the waves;
    you crossed the deep sea,
    but your footprints could not be seen.
²⁰ You led your people like a shepherd,
    with Moses and Aaron in charge.

God and His People^o

78 Listen, my people, to my
        teaching,
    and pay attention to what I say.
² I am going to use wise sayings
    and explain mysteries from the past,
³   things we have heard and known,
    things that our fathers told us.
⁴ We will not keep them from our
        children;
    we will tell the next generation
    about the LORD's power and his great
        deeds
    and the wonderful things he has
        done.

⁵ He gave laws to the people of Israel
    and commandments to the
        descendants of Jacob.
 He instructed our ancestors
    to teach his laws to their children,
⁶ so that the next generation might learn
        them
    and in turn should tell their children.
⁷ In this way they also will put their trust
    in God
    and not forget what he has done,
    but always obey his commandments.
⁸ They will not be like their ancestors,
    a rebellious and disobedient people,
 whose trust in God was never firm
    and who did not remain faithful to
        him.

^o HEBREW TITLE: *A poem by Asaph.*

⁹ The Ephraimites, armed with bows and
    arrows,
  ran away on the day of battle.
¹⁰ They did not keep their covenant with
    God;
  they refused to obey his law.
¹¹ They forgot what he had done,
  the miracles they had seen him
    perform.
¹² While their ancestors watched, God
    performed miracles
  in the plain of Zoan in the land of
    Egypt.
¹³ He divided the sea and took them
    through it;
  he made the waters stand like walls.
¹⁴ By day he led them with a cloud
  and all night long with the light of a
    fire.
¹⁵ He split rocks open in the desert
  and gave them water from the depths.
¹⁶ He caused a stream to come out of the
    rock
  and made water flow like a river.

¹⁷ But they continued to sin against God,
  and in the desert they rebelled against
    the Most High.
¹⁸ They deliberately put God to the test
  by demanding the food they wanted.
¹⁹ They spoke against God and said,
  "Can God supply food in the desert?
²⁰ It is true that he struck the rock,
  and water flowed out in a torrent;
 but can he also provide us with bread
  and give his people meat?"

²¹ And so the LORD was angry when he
    heard them;
  he attacked his people with fire,
  and his anger against them grew,

²² because they had no faith in him
        and did not believe that he would
            save them.
²³ But he spoke to the sky above
        and commanded its doors to open;
²⁴ he gave them grain from heaven,
        by sending down manna for them to
            eat.
²⁵ So they ate the food of angels,
        and God gave them all they wanted.
²⁶ He also caused the east wind to blow,
        and by his power he stirred up the
            south wind;
²⁷ and to his people he sent down birds,
        as many as the grains of sand on the
            shore;
²⁸ they fell in the middle of the camp
        all around the tents.
²⁹ So the people ate and were satisfied;
        God gave them what they wanted.
³⁰ But they had not yet satisfied their
            craving
        and were still eating,
³¹ when God became angry with them
        and killed their strongest men,
        the best young men of Israel.

³² In spite of all this the people kept
            sinning;
        in spite of his miracles they did not
            trust him.
³³ So he ended their days like a breath
        and their lives with sudden disaster.
³⁴ Whenever he killed some of them,
        the rest would turn to him;
        they would repent and pray earnestly
            to him.
³⁵ They remembered that God was their
            protector,
        that the Almighty came to their aid.
³⁶ But their words were all lies;
        nothing they said was sincere.

³⁷ They were not loyal to him;
  they were not faithful to their
    covenant with him.

³⁸ But God was merciful to his people.
  He forgave their sin
  and did not destroy them.
Many times he held back his anger
  and restrained his fury.
³⁹ He remembered that they were only
    mortal beings,
  like a wind that blows by and is gone.

⁴⁰ How often they rebelled against him in
    the desert;
  how many times they made him sad!
⁴¹ Again and again they put God to the
    test
  and brought pain to the Holy God of
    Israel.
⁴² They forgot his great power
  and the day when he saved them
    from their enemies
⁴³   and performed his mighty acts and
    miracles
  in the plain of Zoan in the land of
    Egypt.
⁴⁴ He turned the rivers into blood,
  and the Egyptians had no water to
    drink.
⁴⁵ He sent flies among them, that
    tormented them,
  and frogs that ruined their land.
⁴⁶ He sent locusts to eat their crops
  and to destroy their fields.
⁴⁷ He killed their grapevines with hail
  and their fig trees with frost.
⁴⁸ He killed their cattle with hail
  and their flocks with lightning.ᵖ

ᵖ hail ... lightning; *or* terrible disease ... deadly plague.

49 He caused them great distress
  by pouring out his anger and fierce
    rage,
  which came as messengers of death.
50 He did not restrain his anger
  or spare their lives,
  but killed them with a plague.
51 He killed the first-born sons
  of all the families of Egypt.

52 Then he led his people out like a
    shepherd
  and guided them through the desert.
53 He led them safely, and they were not
    afraid;
  but the sea came rolling over their
    enemies.
54 He brought them to his holy land,
  to the mountains which he himself
    conquered.
55 He drove out the inhabitants as his
    people advanced;
  he divided their land among the
    tribes of Israel
  and gave their homes to his people.

56 But they rebelled against Almighty God
  and put him to the test.
  They did not obey his commandments,
57   but were rebellious and disloyal like
    their fathers,
  unreliable as a crooked arrow.
58 They angered him with their heathen
    places of worship,
  and with their idols they made him
    furious.
59 God was angry when he saw it,
  so he rejected his people completely.
60 He abandoned his tent in Shiloh,*q*
  the home where he had lived among
    us.

q SHILOH: *The central place of worship for the people of Israel before the time of King David.*

61 He allowed our enemies to capture the
      Covenant Box,
    the symbol of his power and glory.
62 He was angry with his own people
    and let them be killed by their
      enemies.
63 Young men were killed in war,
    and young women had no one to
      marry.
64 Priests died by violence,
    and their widows were not allowed to
      mourn.

65 At last the Lord woke up as though
      from sleep;
    he was like a strong man excited by
      wine.
66 He drove his enemies back
    in lasting and shameful defeat.
67 But he rejected the descendants of
      Joseph;
    he did not select the tribe of
      Ephraim.
68 Instead he chose the tribe of Judah
    and Mount Zion, which he dearly
      loves.
69 There he built his Temple
    like his home in heaven;
  he made it firm like the earth itself,
    secure for all time.

70 He chose his servant David;
    he took him from the pastures,
71   where he looked after his flocks,
    and he made him king of Israel,
    the shepherd of the people of God.
72 David took care of them with unselfish
      devotion
    and led them with skill.

A Prayer for the Nation's Deliverance[r]

79 O God, the heathen have invaded
your land.
They have desecrated your holy
Temple
and left Jerusalem in ruins.
2 They left the bodies of your people for
the vultures,
the bodies of your servants for wild
animals to eat.
3 They shed your people's blood like
water;
blood flowed like water all through
Jerusalem,
and no one was left to bury the dead.
4 The surrounding nations insult us;
they laugh at us and mock us.

5 LORD, will you be angry with us
forever?
Will your anger continue to burn like
fire?
6 Turn your anger on the nations that do
not worship you,
on the people who do not pray to
you.
7 For they have killed your people;
they have ruined your country.

8 Do not punish us for the sins of our
ancestors.
Have mercy on us now;
we have lost all hope.
9 Help us, O God, and save us;
rescue us and forgive our sins
for the sake of your own honor.
10 Why should the nations ask us,
"Where is your God?"
Let us see you punish the nations
for shedding the blood of your
servants.

[r] HEBREW TITLE: *A psalm by Asaph.*

¹¹ Listen to the groans of the prisoners,
  and by your great power free those
   who are condemned to die.
¹² Lord, pay the other nations back seven
    times
  for all the insults they have hurled at
   you.
¹³ Then we, your people, the sheep of
   your flock,
  will thank you forever
  and praise you for all time to come.

A Prayer for the Nation's Restoration*

80 Listen to us, O Shepherd of
     Israel;
  hear us, leader of your flock.
Seated on your throne above the
   winged creatures,
² reveal yourself to the tribes of
   Ephraim, Benjamin, and Manasseh.
Show us your strength;
  come and save us!

³ Bring us back, O God!
  Show us your mercy, and we will be
   saved!

⁴ How much longer, LORD God
    Almighty,
  will you be angry with your people's
   prayers?
⁵ You have given us sorrow to eat,
  a large cup of tears to drink.
⁶ You let the surrounding nations fight
   over our land;
  our enemies insult us.

⁷ Bring us back, Almighty God!
  Show us your mercy, and we will be
   saved!

* HEBREW TITLE: *A psalm by Asaph; a testimony.*

8 You brought a grapevine out of Egypt;
   you drove out other nations and
      planted it in their land.
9 You cleared a place for it to grow;
   its roots went deep, and it spread out
      over the whole land.
10 It covered the hills with its shade;
   its branches overshadowed the giant
      cedars.
11 It extended its branches to the
      Mediterranean Sea
   and as far as the Euphrates River.
12 Why did you break down the fences
      around it?
   Now anyone passing by can steal its
      grapes;
13   wild hogs trample it down,
   and wild animals feed on it.

14 Turn to us, Almighty God!
   Look down from heaven at us;
   come and save your people!
15 Come and save this grapevine that you
      planted,
   this young vine you made grow so
      strong!

16 Our enemies have set it on fire and cut
      it down;
   look at them in anger and destroy
      them!
17 Preserve and protect the people you
      have chosen,
   the nation you made so strong.
18 We will never turn away from you
      again;
   keep us alive, and we will praise you.

19 Bring us back, LORD God Almighty.
   Show us your mercy, and we will be
      saved.

A Song for a Festival'

81 Shout for joy to God our
defender;
sing praise to the God of Jacob!

2 Start the music and beat the
tambourines;
play pleasant music on the harps and
the lyres.

3 Blow the trumpet for the festival,
when the moon is new and when the
moon is full.

4 This is the law in Israel,
an order from the God of Jacob.

5 He gave it to the people of Israel
when he attacked the land of Egypt.

I hear an unknown voice saying,

6 "I took the burdens off your backs;
I let you put down your loads of
bricks.

7 When you were in trouble, you called
to me, and I saved you.
From my hiding place in the storm, I
answered you.
I put you to the test at the springs of
Meribah.

8 Listen, my people, to my warning;
Israel, how I wish you would listen to
me!

9 You must never worship another god.

10 I am the LORD your God,
who brought you out of Egypt.
Open your mouth, and I will feed you.

11 "But my people would not listen to me;
Israel would not obey me.

12 So I let them go their stubborn ways
and do whatever they wanted.

' HEBREW TITLE: *By Asaph.*

13 How I wish my people would listen to
    me;
  how I wish they would obey me!
14 I would quickly defeat their enemies
  and conquer all their foes.
15 Those who hate me would bow in fear
    before me;
  their punishment would last forever.
16 But I would feed you with the finest
    wheat
  and satisfy you with wild honey."

God the Supreme Ruler[u]

82 God presides in the heavenly
    council;
  in the assembly of the gods he gives
    his decision:
2 "You must stop judging unjustly;
  you must no longer be partial to the
    wicked!
3 Defend the rights of the poor and the
    orphans;
  be fair to the needy and the helpless.
4 Rescue them from the power of evil
    men.

5 "How ignorant you are! How stupid!
  You are completely corrupt,
  and justice has disappeared from the
    world.
6 'You are gods,' I said;
  'all of you are sons of the Most High.'
7 But you will die like men;
  your life will end like that of any
    prince."

8 Come, O God, and rule the world;
  all the nations are yours.

[u] HEBREW TITLE: *A psalm by Asaph.*

A Prayer for the Defeat of Israel's Enemies[v]

83

O God, do not keep silent;
do not be still, do not be quiet!
[2] Look! Your enemies are in revolt,
and those who hate you are rebelling.
[3] They are making secret plans against
your people;
they are plotting against those you
protect.
[4] "Come," they say, "let us destroy their
nation,
so that Israel will be forgotten
forever."

[5] They agree on their plan
and form an alliance against you:
[6] the people of Edom and the
Ishmaelites;
the people of Moab and the Hagrites;
[7] the people of Gebal, Ammon, and
Amalek,
and of Philistia and Tyre.
[8] Assyria has also joined them
as a strong ally of the Ammonites
and Moabites, the descendants of
Lot.

[9] Do to them what you did to the
Midianites,
and to Sisera and Jabin at the Kishon
River.
[10] You defeated them at Endor,
and their bodies rotted on the ground.
[11] Do to their leaders what you did to
Oreb and Zeeb;
defeat all their rulers as you did
Zebah and Zalmunna,
[12] who said, "We will take for our own
the land that belongs to God."

[13] Scatter them like dust, O God,
like straw blown away by the wind.

[v] HEBREW TITLE: *A psalm by Asaph; a song.*

14 As fire burns the forest,
  as flames set the hills on fire,
15 chase them away with your storm
  and terrify them with your fierce
    winds.
16 Cover their faces with shame, O LORD,
  and make them acknowledge your
    power.
17 May they be defeated and terrified
    forever;
  may they die in complete disgrace.
18 May they know that you alone are the
    LORD,
  supreme ruler over all the earth.

Longing for God's House[w]

84 How I love your Temple, LORD
    Almighty!
2   How I want to be there!
  I long to be in the LORD's Temple.
With my whole being I sing for joy
  to the living God.
3 Even the sparrows have built a nest,
  and the swallows have their own
    home;
they keep their young near your altars,
  LORD Almighty, my king and my
    God.
4 How happy are those who live in your
    Temple,
  always singing praise to you.

5 How happy are those whose strength
    comes from you,
  who are eager to make the pilgrimage
    to Mount Zion.
6 As they pass through the dry valley of
    Baca,
  it becomes a place of springs;
  the early rain fills it with pools.

[w] HEBREW TITLE: *A psalm by the clan of Korah.*

⁷ They grow stronger as they go;
    they will see the God of gods on
      Zion.

⁸ Hear my prayer, LORD God Almighty.
    Listen, O God of Jacob!
⁹ Bless our king, O God,
    the king you have chosen.

¹⁰ One day spent in your Temple
    is better than a thousand anywhere
      else;
  I would rather stand at the gate of the
      house of my God
    than live in the homes of the wicked.
¹¹ The LORD is our protector and glorious
      king,
    blessing us with kindness and honor.
  He does not refuse any good thing
    to those who do what is right.
¹² LORD Almighty, how happy are those
    who trust in you!

A Prayer for the Nation's Welfare ˣ

85 LORD, you have been merciful to
      your land;
  you have made Israel prosperous
      again.
² You have forgiven your people's sins
    and pardoned all their wrongs.
³ You stopped being angry with them
    and held back your furious rage.

⁴ Bring us back, O God our savior,
    and stop being displeased with us!
⁵ Will you be angry with us forever?
    Will your anger never cease?
⁶ Make us strong again,
    and we, your people, will praise you.

ˣ HEBREW TITLE: *A psalm by the clan of Korah.*

7 Show us your constant love, O LORD,
    and give us your saving help.

8 I am listening to what the LORD God is
    saying;
    he promises peace to us, his own
    people,
    if we do not go back to our foolish
    ways.
9 Surely he is ready to save those who
    honor him,
    and his saving presence will remain
    in our land.

10 Love and faithfulness will meet;
    righteousness and peace will embrace.
11 Man's loyalty will reach up from the
    earth,
    and God's righteousness will look
    down from heaven.
12 The LORD will make us prosperous,
    and our land will produce rich
    harvests.
13 Righteousness will go before the LORD
    and prepare the path for him.

A Prayer for Help [y]

86 Listen to me, LORD, and answer
    me,
    for I am helpless and weak.
2 Save me from death, because I am loyal
    to you;
    save me, for I am your servant and I
    trust in you.

3 You are my God, so be merciful to me;
    I pray to you all day long.
4 Make your servant glad, O Lord,
    because my prayers go up to you.

[y] HEBREW TITLE: *A prayer by David.*

5 You are good to us and forgiving,
   full of constant love for all who pray
   to you.

6 Listen, LORD, to my prayer;
   hear my cries for help.
7 I call to you in times of trouble,
   because you answer my prayers.

8 There is no god like you, O Lord,
   not one has done what you have
   done.
9 All the nations that you have created
   will come and bow down to you;
   they will praise your greatness.
10 You are mighty and do wonderful
   things;
   you alone are God.

11 Teach me, LORD, what you want me to
   do,
   and I will obey you faithfully;
   teach me to serve you with complete
   devotion.
12 I will praise you with all my heart, O
   Lord my God;
   I will proclaim your greatness
   forever.
13 How great is your constant love for me!
   You have saved me from the grave
   itself.
14 Proud men are coming against me, O
   God;
   a gang of cruel men is trying to kill
   me—
   people who pay no attention to you.
15 But you, O Lord, are a merciful and
   loving God,
   always patient, always kind and
   faithful.

16 Turn to me and have mercy on me;
  strengthen me and save me,
  because I serve you just as my
    mother did.
17 Show me proof of your goodness,
    LORD;
  those who hate me will be ashamed
  when they see that you have given
    me comfort and help.

In Praise of Jerusalem [z]

87 The LORD built his city on the
    sacred hill; [a]
2   more than any other place in Israel
  he loves the city of Jerusalem.
3 Listen, city of God,
  to the wonderful things he says about
    you:

4 "I will include Egypt and Babylonia
  when I list the nations that obey me;
 the people of Philistia, Tyre, and Sudan
  I will number among the inhabitants
    of Jerusalem."

5 Of Zion it will be said
  that all nations belong there
  and that the Almighty will make her
    strong.
6 The LORD will write a list of the
    peoples
  and include them all as citizens of
    Jerusalem.
7 They dance and sing,
  "In Zion is the source of all our
    blessings."

[z] HEBREW TITLE: *A psalm by the clan of Korah; a song.* [a] SACRED
HILL: *See 2.6.*

A Cry for Help[b]

88 LORD God, my savior, I cry out
          all day,
    and at night I come before you.
2 Hear my prayer;
    listen to my cry for help!

3 So many troubles have fallen on me
    that I am close to death.
4 I am like all others who are about to
          die;
    all my strength is gone.[c]
5 I am abandoned among the dead;
    I am like the slain lying in their
          graves,
  those you have forgotten completely,
    who are beyond your help.
6 You have thrown me into the depths of
          the tomb,
    into the darkest and deepest pit.
7 Your anger lies heavy on me,
    and I am crushed beneath its waves.

8 You have caused my friends to abandon
          me;
    you have made me repulsive to them.
  I am closed in and cannot escape;
9   my eyes are weak from suffering.
  LORD, every day I call to you
    and lift my hands to you in prayer.

10 Do you perform miracles for the dead?
    Do they rise up and praise you?
11 Is your constant love spoken of in the
          grave
    or your faithfulness in the place of
          destruction?

---

[b] HEBREW TITLE: *A psalm by the clan of Korah; a song. A poem by Heman the Ezrahite.*   [c] all my strength is gone; *or* there is no help for me.

12 Are your miracles seen in that place of
    darkness
      or your goodness in the land of the
        forgotten?

13 LORD, I call to you for help;
     every morning I pray to you.
14 Why do you reject me, LORD?
     Why do you turn away from me?
15 Ever since I was young, I have suffered
     and been near death;
   I am worn out[d] from the burden of
     your punishments.
16 Your furious anger crushes me;
     your terrible attacks destroy me.
17 All day long they surround me like a
     flood;
   they close in on me from every side.
18 You have made even my closest friends
     abandon me,
   and darkness is my only companion.

A Hymn in Time of National Trouble[e]

89 O LORD, I will always sing of
     your constant love;
   I will proclaim your faithfulness
     forever.
2 I know that your love will last for all
    time,
   that your faithfulness is as permanent
     as the sky.
3 You said, "I have made a covenant
     with the man I chose;
   I have promised my servant David,
4 'A descendant of yours will always be
     king;
   I will preserve your dynasty
     forever.' "

---

[d] Probable text I am worn out; Hebrew unclear.   [e] HEBREW TITLE: A
poem by Ethan the Ezrahite.

⁵ The heavens sing of the wonderful
    things you do;
  the holy ones sing of your
    faithfulness, LORD.
⁶ No one in heaven is like you, LORD;
  none of the heavenly beings is your
    equal.
⁷ You are feared in the council of the
    holy ones;
  they all stand in awe of you.

⁸ LORD God Almighty, none is as mighty
    as you;
  in all things you are faithful, O LORD.
⁹ You rule over the powerful sea;
  you calm its angry waves.
¹⁰ You crushed the monster Rahab*f* and
    killed it;
  with your mighty strength you
    defeated your enemies.
¹¹ Heaven is yours, the earth also;
  you made the world and everything
    in it.
¹² You created the north and the south;
  Mount Tabor and Mount Hermon
    sing to you for joy.
¹³ How powerful you are!
  How great is your strength!
¹⁴ Your kingdom is founded on
    righteousness and justice;
  love and faithfulness are shown in all
    you do.

¹⁵ How happy are the people who
    worship you with songs,
  who live in the light of your kindness!
¹⁶ Because of you they rejoice all day
    long,
  and they praise you for your
    goodness.
¹⁷ You give us great victories;
  in your love you make us triumphant.

f RAHAB: *A legendary sea monster which represented the forces of chaos and evil.*

18 You, O LORD, chose our protector;
   you, the Holy God of Israel, gave us
   our king.

God's Promise to David

19 In a vision long ago you said to your
   faithful servants,
   "I have given help to a famous
   soldier;
   I have given the throne to one I
   chose from the people.
20 I have made my servant David king
   by anointing him with holy oil.
21 My strength will always be with him,
   my power will make him strong.
22 His enemies will never succeed against
   him;
   the wicked will not defeat him.
23 I will crush his foes
   and kill everyone who hates him.
24 I will love him and be loyal to him;
   I will make him always victorious.
25 I will extend his kingdom
   from the Mediterranean to the
   Euphrates River.
26 He will say to me,
   'You are my father and my God;
   you are my protector and savior.'
27 I will make him my first-born son,
   the greatest of all kings.
28 I will always keep my promise to him,
   and my covenant with him will last
   forever.
29 His dynasty will be as permanent as the
   sky;
   a descendant of his will always be
   king.

30 "But if his descendants disobey my law
   and do not live according to my
   commands,

³¹ if they disregard my instructions
    and do not keep my commandments,
³² then I will punish them for their sins;
    I will make them suffer for their
        wrongs.
³³ But I will not stop loving David
    or fail to keep my promise to him.
³⁴ I will not break my covenant with him
    or take back even one promise I
        made him.

³⁵ "Once and for all I have promised by
        my holy name:
    I will never lie to David.
³⁶ He will always have descendants,
    and I will watch over his kingdom as
        long as the sun shines.
³⁷ It will be as permanent as the moon,
    that faithful witness in the sky."

Lament over the Defeat of the King

³⁸ But you are angry with your chosen
        king;
    you have deserted and rejected him.
³⁹ You have broken your covenant with
        your servant
    and thrown his crown in the dirt.
⁴⁰ You have torn down the walls of his
        city
    and left his forts in ruins.
⁴¹ All who pass by steal his belongings;
    all his neighbors laugh at him.
⁴² You have given the victory to his
        enemies;
    you have made them all happy.
⁴³ You have made his weapons useless
    and let him be defeated in battle.
⁴⁴ You have taken away his royal scepter[g]
    and knocked his throne to the
        ground.

[g] *Probable text* royal scepter; *Hebrew* purity.

⁴⁵ You have made him old before his time
   and covered him with disgrace.

A Prayer for Deliverance

⁴⁶ LORD, will you hide yourself forever?
      How long will your anger burn like
      fire?
⁴⁷ Remember how short my life is;
      remember that you created all of us
      mortal!
⁴⁸ Who can live and never die?
      How can man keep himself from the
      grave?

⁴⁹ Lord, where are the former proofs of
      your love?
      Where are the promises you made to
      David?
⁵⁰ Don't forget how I, your servant, am
      insulted,
      how I endure all the curses *h* of the
      heathen.
⁵¹ Your enemies insult your chosen king,
      O LORD!
      They insult him wherever he goes.

⁵² Praise the LORD forever!

      Amen! Amen!

BOOK FOUR
(Psalms 90—106)

Of God and Man *i*

90   O Lord, you have always been
          our home.
² Before you created the hills
      or brought the world into being,
      you were eternally God,
      and will be God forever

---

h *Probable text* curses; *Hebrew* crowds.   *i* HEBREW TITLE: *A prayer
by Moses, the man of God.*

³ You tell man to return to what he was;
  you change him back to dust.
⁴ A thousand years to you are like one
      day;
    they are like yesterday, already gone,
    like a short hour in the night.
⁵ You carry us away like a flood;
    we last no longer than a dream.
  We are like weeds that sprout in the
      morning,
⁶   that grow and burst into bloom,
    then dry up and die in the evening.

⁷ We are destroyed by your anger;
    we are terrified by your fury.
⁸ You place our sins before you,
    our secret sins where you can see
      them.

⁹ Our life is cut short by your anger;
    it fades away like a whisper.
¹⁰ Seventy years is all we have—
    eighty years, if we are strong;
  yet all they bring us is trouble and
      sorrow;
    life is soon over, and we are gone.

¹¹ Who has felt the full power of your
      anger?
    Who knows what fear your fury can
      bring?
¹² Teach us how short our life is,
    so that we may become wise.

¹³ How much longer will your anger last?
    Have pity, O LORD, on your servants!
¹⁴ Fill us each morning with your
      constant love,
    so that we may sing and be glad all
      our life.
¹⁵ Give us now as much happiness as the
      sadness you gave us
    during all our years of misery.

¹⁶ Let us, your servants, see your mighty
> deeds;
> let our descendants see your glorious
> might,
¹⁷ LORD our God, may your blessings be
> with us.
> Give us success in all we do!

God Our Protector

91 Whoever goes to the LORD for
> safety,
> whoever remains under the
> protection of the Almighty,
² can say to him,
> "You are my defender and protector.
> You are my God; in you I trust."
³ He will keep you safe from all hidden
> dangers
> and from all deadly diseases.
⁴ He will cover you with his wings;
> you will be safe in his care;
> his faithfulness will protect and
> defend you.
⁵ You need not fear any dangers at night
> or sudden attacks during the day
⁶ or the plagues that strike in the dark
> or the evils that kill in daylight.

⁷ A thousand may fall dead beside you,
> ten thousand all around you,
> but you will not be harmed.
⁸ You will look and see
> how the wicked are punished.

⁹ You have made the LORD your*
> defender,
> the Most High your protector,
¹⁰ and so no disaster will strike you,
> no violence will come near your
> home.

* *Probable text* your; *Hebrew* my.

¹¹ God will put his angels in charge of
　　you
　　to protect you wherever you go.
¹² They will hold you up with their hands
　　to keep you from hurting your feet on
　　the stones.
¹³ You will trample down lions and
　　snakes,
　　fierce lions and poisonous snakes.

¹⁴ God says, "I will save those who love
　　me
　　and will protect those who
　　acknowledge me as LORD.
¹⁵ When they call to me, I will answer
　　them;
　　when they are in trouble, I will be
　　with them.
　　I will rescue them and honor them.
¹⁶ I will reward them with long life;
　　I will save them."

A Song of Praise[J]

92　　How good it is to give thanks to
　　　　you, O LORD,
　　to sing in your honor, O Most High
　　God,
² to proclaim your constant love every
　　morning
　　and your faithfulness every night,
³ with the music of stringed instruments
　　and with melody on the harp.
⁴ Your mighty deeds, O LORD, make me
　　glad;
　　because of what you have done, I
　　sing for joy.

⁵ How great are your actions, LORD!
　　How deep are your thoughts!

[J] HEBREW TITLE: *A psalm; a song for the Sabbath.*

⁶ This is something a fool cannot know;
  a stupid man cannot understand:
⁷ the wicked may grow like weeds,
  those who do wrong may prosper;
yet they will be totally destroyed,
⁸   because you, LORD, are supreme
     forever.

⁹ We know that your enemies will die,
  and all the wicked will be defeated.
¹⁰ You have made me as strong as a wild
   ox;
   you have blessed me with happiness.
¹¹ I have seen the defeat of my enemies
   and heard the cries of the wicked.

¹² The righteous will flourish like palm
   trees;
   they will grow like the cedars of
   Lebanon.
¹³ They are like trees planted in the house
   of the LORD,
   that flourish in the Temple of our
   God,
¹⁴   that still bear fruit in old age
      and are always green and strong.
¹⁵ This shows that the LORD is just,
   that there is no wrong in my
   protector.

God the King

93 The LORD is king.
         He is clothed with majesty and
         strength.
   The earth is set firmly in place
   and cannot be moved.
² Your throne, O LORD, has been firm
  from the beginning,
  and you existed before time began.

³ The ocean depths raise their voice, O
  LORD;
  they raise their voice and roar.

⁴ The LORD rules supreme in heaven,
    greater than the roar of the ocean,
    more powerful than the waves of the
       sea.

⁵ Your laws are eternal, LORD,
    and your Temple is holy indeed,
    forever and ever.

God the Judge of All

94 LORD, you are a God who
        punishes;
    reveal your anger!
² You are the judge of all men;
    rise and give the proud what they
       deserve!
³ How much longer will the wicked be
       glad?
    How much longer, LORD?
⁴ How much longer will criminals be
       proud
    and boast about their crimes?

⁵ They crush your people, LORD;
    they oppress those who belong to
       you.
⁶ They kill widows and orphans,
    and murder the strangers who live in
       our land.
⁷ They say, "The LORD does not see us;
    the God of Israel does not notice."

⁸ My people, how can you be such stupid
       fools?
    When will you ever learn?
⁹ God made our ears—can't he hear?
    He made our eyes—can't he see?
¹⁰ He scolds the nations—won't he punish
       them?[x]
    He is the teacher of all men—hasn't
    he any knowledge?

[x] them?; *or* our wicked leaders?

11 The LORD knows what they think;
   he knows how senseless their
     reasoning is.

12 LORD, how happy is the person you
     instruct,
   the one to whom you teach your law!
13 You give him rest from days of trouble
   until a pit is dug to trap the wicked.
14 The LORD will not abandon his people;
   he will not desert those who belong
     to him.
15 Justice will again be found in the
     courts,
   and all righteous people will support
     it.

16 Who stood up for me against the
     wicked?
   Who took my side against the
     evildoers?
17 If the LORD had not helped me,
   I would have gone quickly to the
     land of silence.[k]
18 I said, "I am falling";
   but your constant love, O LORD, held
     me up.
19 Whenever I am anxious and worried,
   you comfort me and make me glad.

20 You have nothing to do with corrupt
     judges,
   who make injustice legal,
21   who plot against good men
   and sentence the innocent to death.
22 But the LORD defends me;
   my God protects me.
23 He will punish them for their
     wickedness
   and destroy them for their sins;
   the LORD our God will destroy them.

[k] LAND OF SILENCE: *The world of the dead (see 6.5).*

A Song of Praise

95 Come, let us praise the LORD!
Let us sing for joy to God, who
protects us!

2 Let us come before him with
thanksgiving
and sing joyful songs of praise.

3 For the LORD is a mighty God,
a mighty king over all the gods.

4 He rules over the whole earth,
from the deepest caves to the highest
hills.

5 He rules over the sea, which he made;
the land also, which he himself
formed.

Let us praise the LORD! (95.1)

⁶ Come, let us bow down and worship
          him;
     let us kneel before the LORD, our
          Maker!
⁷ He is our God;
     we are the people he cares for,
     the flock for which he provides.

Listen today to what he says:
⁸ "Don't be stubborn, as your ancestors
          were at Meribah,
     as they were that day in the desert at
          Massah.
⁹ There they put me to the test and tried
          me,
     although they had seen what I did for
          them.
¹⁰ For forty years I was disgusted with
          those people.
     I said, 'How disloyal they are!
     They refuse to obey my commands.'
¹¹ I was angry and made a solemn
          promise:
     'You will never enter the land
     where I would have given you rest.' "

God the Supreme King
(1 Chronicles 16.23-33)

96 Sing a new song to the LORD!
          Sing to the LORD, all the world!
² Sing to the LORD, and praise him!
     Proclaim every day the good news
          that he has saved us.
³ Proclaim his glory to the nations,
     his mighty deeds to all peoples.

⁴ The LORD is great and is to be highly
          praised;
     he is to be honored more than all the
          gods.

⁵ The gods of all other nations are only
   idols,
   but the LORD created the heavens.
⁶ Glory and majesty surround him;
   power and beauty fill his Temple.

⁷ Praise the LORD, all people on earth;
   praise his glory and might.
⁸ Praise the LORD's glorious name;
   bring an offering and come into his
   Temple.
⁹ Bow down before the Holy One when
   he appears;[1]
   tremble before him, all the earth!

¹⁰ Say to all the nations, "The LORD is
    king!
    The earth is set firmly in place and
    cannot be moved;
    he will judge the peoples with
    justice."
¹¹ Be glad, earth and sky!
    Roar, sea, and every creature in you;
¹²   be glad, fields, and everything in you!
    The trees in the woods will shout for
    joy
¹³   when the LORD comes to rule the
    earth.
    He will rule the peoples of the world
    with justice and fairness.

God the Supreme Ruler

97 The LORD is king! Earth, be glad!
   Rejoice, you islands of the seas!
² Clouds and darkness surround him;
   he rules with righteousness and
   justice.
³ Fire goes in front of him
   and burns up his enemies around
   him.

---

[1] when he appears; *or* in garments of worship.

4 His lightning lights up the world;
  the earth sees it and trembles.
5 The hills melt like wax before the
      LORD,
    before the Lord of all the earth.
6 The heavens proclaim his righteousness,
    and all the nations see his glory.

7 Everyone who worships idols is put to
      shame;
    all the gods bow down[m] before the
      LORD.
8 The people of Zion are glad,
    and the cities of Judah rejoice
    because of your judgments, O LORD.
9 LORD Almighty, you are ruler of all the
      earth;
    you are much greater than all the
      gods.

10 The LORD loves those who hate evil;[n]
    he protects the lives of his people;
    he rescues them from the power of
      the wicked.
11 Light shines on the righteous,
    and gladness on the good.
12 All you that are righteous be glad
    because of what the LORD has done!
  Remember what the holy God has
      done,
    and give thanks to him.

God the Ruler of the World[x]

98 Sing a new song to the LORD;
      he has done wonderful things!
  By his own power and holy strength
    he has won the victory.

---

[m] all the gods bow down; *or* bow down, all gods.   [n] *Probable text*
The LORD loves those who hate evil; *Hebrew* Hate evil, you who
love the LORD.   [x] HEBREW TITLE: *A psalm.*

2 The LORD announced his victory;
>   he made his saving power known to
>   the nations.
3 He kept his promise to the people of
>   Israel
>   with loyalty and constant love for
>   them.
> All people everywhere have seen the
>   victory of our God.

4 Sing for joy to the LORD, all the earth;
>   praise him with songs and shouts of
>   joy!
5 Sing praises to the LORD!
> Play music on the harps!
6 Blow trumpets and horns,
>   and shout for joy to the LORD, our
>   king.

7 Roar, sea, and every creature in you;
>   sing, earth, and all who live on you!
8 Clap your hands, you rivers;
>   you hills, sing together with joy
>   before the LORD,
9   because he comes to rule the earth.
> He will rule the peoples of the world
>   with justice and fairness.

God the Supreme King

99 The LORD is king,
>   and the people tremble.
> He sits on his throne above the winged
>   creatures,
>   and the earth shakes.
2 The LORD is mighty in Zion;
>   he is supreme over all the nations.
3 Everyone will praise his great and
>   majestic name.
> Holy is he!

4 Mighty king,^o you love what is right;
  you have established justice in Israel;
  you have brought righteousness and
    fairness.
5 Praise the LORD our God;
  worship before his throne!
  Holy is he!

6 Moses and Aaron were his priests,
  and Samuel was one who prayed to
    him;
  they called to the LORD, and he
    answered them.
7 He spoke to them from the pillar of
    cloud;
  they obeyed the laws and commands
    that he gave them.

8 O LORD, our God, you answered your
    people;
  you showed them that you are a God
    who forgives,
  even though you punished them for
    their sins.
9 Praise the LORD our God,
  and worship at his sacred hill!^p
The LORD our God is holy.

A Hymn of Praise^q

100 Sing to the LORD, all the
         world!
2 Worship the LORD with joy;
  come before him with happy songs!

3 Acknowledge that the LORD is God.
  He made us, and we belong to him;
  we are his people, we are his flock.

---

^o *Probable text* Mighty king; *Hebrew* The might of the king.
^p SACRED HILL: *See 2.6.*   ^q HEBREW TITLE: *A psalm of thanksgiving.*

4 Enter the Temple gates with
    thanksgiving;
    go into its courts with praise.
    Give thanks to him and praise him.

5 The LORD is good;
    his love is eternal
    and his faithfulness lasts forever.

A King's Promise*

101   My song is about loyalty and
              justice,
    and I sing it to you, O LORD.
2 My conduct will be faultless.
    When will you come to me?

I will live a pure life in my house
3   and will never tolerate evil.
I hate the actions of those who turn
    away from God;
    I will have nothing to do with them.
4 I will not be dishonest*
    and will have no dealings with evil.*
5 I will get rid of anyone
    who whispers evil things about
        someone else;
 I will not tolerate a man
    who is proud and arrogant.

6 I will approve of those who are faithful
        to God
    and will let them live in my palace.
Those who are completely honest
    will be allowed to serve me.

7 No liar will live in my palace;
    no hypocrite will remain in my
        presence.

---

* HEBREW TITLE: *A psalm by David.*   *not be dishonest; or* stay
away from dishonest people.   *evil; or* evil men.

⁸ Day after day I will destroy
the wicked in our land;
I will expel all evil men
from the city of the LORD.

The Prayer of a Troubled Young Man ᵘ

102 Listen to my prayer, O LORD,
and hear my cry for help!
² When I am in trouble,
don't turn away from me!
Listen to me,
and answer me quickly when I call!

³ My life is disappearing like smoke;
my body is burning like fire.
⁴ I am beaten down like dry grass;
I have lost my desire for food.
⁵ I groan aloud;
I am nothing but skin and bones.
⁶ I am like a wild bird in the desert,
like an owl in abandoned ruins.
⁷ I lie awake;
I am like a lonely bird on a housetop.
⁸ All day long my enemies insult me;
those who mock me use my name in
cursing.

⁹⁻¹⁰ Because of your anger and fury,
ashes are my food,
and my tears are mixed with my
drink.
You picked me up and threw me away.
¹¹ My life is like the evening shadows;
I am like dry grass.

¹² But you, O LORD, are king forever;
all generations will remember you.

ᵘ HEBREW TITLE: *A prayer by a weary sufferer who pours out his
complaints to the LORD.*

¹³ You will rise and take pity on Zion;
    the time has come to have mercy on
      her;
    this is the right time.
¹⁴ Your servants love her,
    even though she is destroyed;
they have pity on her,
    even though she is in ruins.

¹⁵ The nations will fear the LORD;
    all the kings of the earth will fear his
      power.
¹⁶ When the LORD rebuilds Zion,
    he will reveal his greatness.
¹⁷ He will hear his abandoned people
    and listen to their prayer.

¹⁸ Write down for the coming generation
    what the LORD has done,
    so that people not yet born will
      praise him.
¹⁹ The LORD looked down from his holy
      place on high,
    he looked down from heaven to
      earth.
²⁰ He heard the groans of prisoners
    and set free those who were
      condemned to die.
²¹ And so his name will be proclaimed in
      Zion,
    and he will be praised in Jerusalem
²²   when nations and kingdoms come
      together
    and worship the LORD.

²³ The LORD has made me weak while I
      am still young;
    he has shortened my life.
²⁴ O God, do not take me away now
    before I grow old.

O LORD, you live forever;

²⁵   long ago you created the earth,
    and with your own hands you made
      the heavens.

²⁶ They will disappear, but you will
    remain;
    they will all wear out like clothes.
    You will discard them like clothes,
    and they will vanish.

²⁷ But you are always the same,
    and your life never ends.

²⁸ Our children will live in safety,
    and under your protection
    their descendants will be secure.

The Love of God ᵛ

103   Praise the LORD, my soul!
      All my being, praise his holy
      name!

² Praise the LORD, my soul,
    and do not forget how kind he is.

³ He forgives all my sins
    and heals all my diseases.

⁴ He keeps me from the grave
    and blesses me with love and mercy.

⁵ He fills my life ʷ with good things,
    so that I stay young and strong like
      an eagle.

⁶ The LORD judges in favor of the
    oppressed
    and gives them their rights.

⁷ He revealed his plans to Moses
    and let the people of Israel see his
      mighty deeds.

⁸ The LORD is merciful and loving,
    slow to become angry and full of
      constant love.

⁹ He does not keep on rebuking;
    he is not angry forever.

ᵛ HEBREW TITLE: *By David.*   ʷ *Probable text* my life; *Hebrew
unclear.*

¹⁰ He does not punish us as we deserve
  or repay us according to our sins and
    wrongs.
¹¹ As high as the sky is above the earth,
    so great is his love for those who
      have reverence for him.
¹² As far as the east is from the west,
    so far does he remove our sins from
      us.
¹³ As a father is kind to his children,
    so the LORD is kind to those who
      honor him.
¹⁴ He knows what we are made of;
    he remembers that we are dust.

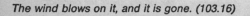

The wind blows on it, and it is gone. (103.16)

15 As for us, our life is like grass.
   We grow and flourish like a wild
      flower;
16   then the wind blows on it, and it is
     gone—
   no one sees it again.
17 But for those who honor the LORD, his
   love lasts forever,
   and his goodness endures for all
     generations
18 of those who are true to his covenant
   and who faithfully obey his
     commands.

19 The LORD placed his throne in heaven;
   he is king over all.
20 Praise the LORD, you strong and mighty
   angels,
   who obey his commands,
   who listen to what he says.
21 Praise the LORD, all you heavenly
   powers,
   you servants of his, who do his will!
22 Praise the LORD, all his creatures
   in all the places he rules.
   Praise the LORD, my soul!

In Praise of the Creator

104   Praise the LORD, my soul!
       O LORD, my God, how great
       you are!
   You are clothed with majesty and glory;
2   you cover yourself with light.
   You spread out the heavens like a tent
3   and built your home on the waters
     above.ˣ
   You use the clouds as your chariot
   and ride on the wings of the wind.

ˣ THE WATERS ABOVE: *A reference to the waters above the celestial
dome (Genesis 1.6–7).*

⁴ You use the winds as your messengers
     and flashes of lightning as your
          servants.

⁵ You have set the earth firmly on its
          foundations,
     and it will never be moved.
⁶ You placed the ocean over it like a
          robe,
     and the water covered the mountains.
⁷ When you rebuked the waters, they
          fled;
     they rushed away when they heard
          your shout of command.
⁸ They flowed over the mountains and
          into the valleys,
     to the place you had made for them.
⁹ You set a boundary they can never
          pass,
     to keep them from covering the earth
          again.

¹⁰ You make springs flow in the valleys,
     and rivers run between the hills.
¹¹ They provide water for the wild
          animals;
     there the wild donkeys quench their
          thirst.
¹² In the trees near by,
     the birds make their nests and sing.

¹³ From the sky you send rain on the hills,
     and the earth is filled with your
          blessings.
¹⁴ You make grass grow for the cattle
     and plants for man to use,
   so that he can grow his crops
¹⁵   and produce wine to make him
          happy,
     olive oil to make him cheerful,
     and bread to give him strength.

You make springs flow in the valleys. (104.10)

16 The cedars of Lebanon get plenty of
        rain—
    the LORD's own trees, which he
        planted.
17 There the birds build their nests;
    the storks nest in the fir trees.
18 The wild goats live in the high
        mountains,
    and the rock badgers hide in the
        cliffs.

19 You created the moon to mark the
        months;
    the sun knows the time to set.
20 You made the night, and in the
        darkness
    all the wild animals come out.
21 The young lions roar while they hunt,
    looking for the food that God
        provides.
22 When the sun rises, they go back
    and lie down in their dens.
23 Then people go out to do their work
    and keep working until evening.

24 LORD, you have made so many things!
    How wisely you made them all!
    The earth is filled with your
        creatures.
25 There is the ocean, large and wide,
    where countless creatures live,
    large and small alike.
26 The ships sail on it, and in it plays
        Leviathan,
    that sea monster which you made.ʸ

27 All of them depend on you
    to give them food when they need it.
28 You give it to them, and they eat it;
    you provide food, and they are
        satisfied.

ʸ in it plays . . . made; or Leviathan is there, that sea monster you
made to amuse you.

29 When you turn away, they are afraid;
   when you take away your breath,
      they die
   and go back to the dust from which
      they came,
30 But when you give them breath,[z] they
      are created;
   you give new life to the earth.

31 May the glory of the LORD last forever!
   May the LORD be happy with what
      he has made!
32 He looks at the earth, and it trembles;
   he touches the mountains, and they
      pour out smoke.

33 I will sing to the LORD all my life;
   as long as I live I will sing praises to
      my God.
34 May he be pleased with my song,
   for my gladness comes from him.
35 May sinners be destroyed from the
      earth;
   may the wicked be no more.

   Praise the LORD, my soul!
   Praise the LORD!

God and His People
(1 Chronicles 16.8-22)

105 Give thanks to the LORD,
            proclaim his greatness;
   tell the nations what he has done.
2 Sing praise to the LORD;
   tell the wonderful things he has done.
3 Be glad that we belong to him;
   let all who worship him rejoice.
4 Go to the LORD for help;
   and worship him continually.

---

[z] give them breath; *or* send out your spirit.

⁵⁻⁶ You descendants of Abraham, his
         servant;
     you descendants of Jacob, the man he
         chose:
   remember the miracles that God
         performed
     and the judgments that he gave.

⁷ The LORD is our God;
     his commands are for all the world.
⁸ He will keep his covenant forever,
     his promises for a thousand
         generations.
⁹ He will keep the agreement he made
         with Abraham
     and his promise to Isaac.
¹⁰ The LORD made a covenant with Jacob,
     one that will last forever.
¹¹ "I will give you the land of Canaan," he
         said.
     "It will be your own possession."

¹² God's people were few in number,
     strangers in the land of Canaan.
¹³ They wandered from country to
         country,
     from one kingdom to another.
¹⁴ But God let no one oppress them;
     to protect them, he warned the kings:
¹⁵ "Don't harm my chosen servants;
     do not touch my prophets."

¹⁶ The LORD sent famine to their country
     and took away all their food.
¹⁷ But he sent a man ahead of them,
     Joseph, who had been sold as a slave.
¹⁸ His feet were kept in chains,
     and an iron collar was around his
         neck,
¹⁹   until what he had predicted came
         true.
   The word of the LORD proved him
         right.

²⁰ Then the king of Egypt had him
      released;
   the ruler of nations set him free.
²¹ He put him in charge of his government
   and made him ruler over all the land,
²²   with power over the king's officials
   and authority to instruct his advisers.

²³ Then Jacob went to Egypt
   and settled in that country.
²⁴ The LORD gave many children to his
      people
   and made them stronger than their
      enemies.
²⁵ He made the Egyptians hate his people
   and treat his servants with deceit.

²⁶ Then he sent his servant Moses,
   and Aaron, whom he had chosen.
²⁷ They did God's mighty acts
   and performed miracles in Egypt.
²⁸ God sent darkness on the country,
   but the Egyptians did not obey[a] his
      command.
²⁹ He turned their rivers into blood
   and killed all their fish.
³⁰ Their country was overrun with frogs;
   even the palace was filled with them.
³¹ God commanded, and flies and gnats
      swarmed throughout the whole
      country.
³² He sent hail and lightning on their land
   instead of rain;
³³ he destroyed their grapevines and fig
      trees
   and broke down all the trees.
³⁴ He commanded, and the locusts came,
   countless millions of them;
³⁵ they ate all the plants in the land;
   they ate all the crops.

[a] *Some ancient translations* did not obey; *Hebrew* obeyed.

³⁶ He killed the first-born sons
  of all the families of Egypt.

³⁷ Then he led the Israelites out;
  they carried silver and gold,
  and all of them were healthy and
    strong.
³⁸ The Egyptians were afraid of them
  and were glad when they left.
³⁹ God put a cloud over his people
  and a fire at night to give them light.
⁴⁰ They *b* asked, and he sent quails;
  he gave them food from heaven to
    satisfy them.
⁴¹ He opened a rock, and water gushed
    out,
  flowing through the desert like a
    river.
⁴² He remembered his sacred promise
  to Abraham his servant.

⁴³ So he led his chosen people out,
  and they sang and shouted for joy.
⁴⁴ He gave them the lands of other
    peoples
  and let them take over their fields,
⁴⁵ so that his people would obey his laws
  and keep all his commands.

Praise the LORD!

The LORD's Goodness to His People

106 Praise the LORD!

Give thanks to the LORD, because he is
    good;
  his love is eternal.
² Who can tell all the great things he has
    done?
  Who can praise him enough?

---

b Some ancient translations They; *Hebrew* He.

³ Happy are those who obey his
    commands,
   who always do what is right.

⁴ Remember me, LORD, when you help
    your people;
   include me when you save them.
⁵ Let me see the prosperity of your
    people
   and share in the happiness of your
    nation,
   in the glad pride of those who belong
    to you.

⁶ We have sinned as our ancestors did;
   we have been wicked and evil.
⁷ Our ancestors in Egypt did not
    understand God's wonderful acts;
   they forgot the many times he
    showed them his love,
   and they rebelled against the
    Almighty*ᶜ* at the Red Sea.
⁸ But he saved them, as he had promised,
   in order to show his great power.
⁹ He gave a command to the Red Sea,
    and it dried up;
   he led his people across on dry land.
¹⁰ He saved them from those who hated
    them;
   he rescued them from their enemies.
¹¹ But the water drowned their enemies;
   not one of them was left.
¹² Then his people believed his promises
   and sang praises to him.

¹³ But they quickly forgot what he had
    done
   and acted without waiting for his
    advice.

ᶜ *Probable text* the Almighty; *Hebrew* the sea.

¹⁴ They were filled with craving in the
desert
and put God to the test;
¹⁵ so he gave them what they asked for,
but also sent a terrible disease among
them.

¹⁶ There in the desert they were jealous of
Moses
and of Aaron, the LORD's holy
servant.
¹⁷ Then the earth opened up and
swallowed Dathan
and buried Abiram and his family;
¹⁸ fire came down on their followers
and burned up those wicked people.

¹⁹ They made a gold bull-calf at Sinai
and worshiped that idol;
²⁰ they exchanged the glory of God
for the image of an animal that eats
grass.
²¹ They forgot the God who had saved
them
by his mighty acts in Egypt.
²² What wonderful things he did there!
What amazing things at the Red Sea!
²³ When God said that he would destroy
his people,
his chosen servant, Moses, stood up
against God
and kept his anger from destroying
them.

²⁴ Then they rejected the pleasant land,
because they did not believe God's
promise.
²⁵ They stayed in their tents and grumbled
and would not listen to the LORD.
²⁶ So he gave them a solemn warning
that he would make them die in the
desert

²⁷ and scatter their descendants among
  the heathen,
  letting them die in foreign countries.

²⁸ Then at Peor, God's people joined in
  the worship of Baal
  and ate sacrifices offered to dead
  gods.
²⁹ They stirred up the LORD's anger by
  their actions,
  and a terrible disease broke out
  among them.
³⁰ But Phinehas stood up and punished
  the guilty,
  and the plague was stopped.
³¹ This has been remembered in his favor
  ever since
  and will be for all time to come.

³² At the springs of Meribah the people
  made the LORD angry,
  and Moses was in trouble on their
  account.
³³ They made him so bitter
  that he spoke without stopping to
  think.

³⁴ They did not kill the heathen,
  as the LORD had commanded them to
  do,
³⁵ but they intermarried with them
  and adopted their pagan ways.
³⁶ God's people worshiped idols,
  and this caused their destruction.
³⁷ They offered their own sons and
  daughters
  as sacrifices to the idols of Canaan.
³⁸ They killed those innocent children,
  and the land was defiled by those
  murders.
³⁹ They made themselves impure by their
  actions
  and were unfaithful to God.

⁴⁰ So the LORD was angry with his people;
   he was disgusted with them.
⁴¹ He abandoned them to the power of the
      heathen,
   and their enemies ruled over them.
⁴² They were oppressed by their enemies
   and were in complete subjection to
      them.
⁴³ Many times the LORD rescued his
      people,
   but they chose to rebel against him
   and sank deeper into sin.
⁴⁴ Yet the LORD heard them when they
      cried out,
   and he took notice of their distress.
⁴⁵ For their sake he remembered his
      covenant,
   and because of his great love he
      relented.
⁴⁶ He made all their oppressors
   feel sorry for them.

⁴⁷ Save us, O LORD our God,
      and bring us back from among the
         nations,
   so that we may be thankful
      and praise your holy name.

⁴⁸ Praise the LORD, the God of Israel
      praise him now and forever!
   Let everyone say, "Amen!"

Praise the LORD!

BOOK FIVE
(Psalms 107—150)

In Praise of God's Goodness

107   "Give thanks to the LORD,
            because he is good;
      his love is eternal!"

2 Repeat these words in praise to the
       LORD,
   all you whom he has saved.
He has rescued you from your enemies
3   and has brought you back from
       foreign countries,
   from east and west, from north and
       south.[d]

4 Some wandered in the trackless desert
   and could not find their way to a city
       to live in.
5 They were hungry and thirsty
   and had given up all hope.
6 Then in their trouble they called to the
       LORD,
   and he saved them from their distress.
7 He led them by a straight road
   to a city where they could live.
8 They must thank the LORD for his
       constant love,
   for the wonderful things he did for
       them.
9 He satisfies those who are thirsty
   and fills the hungry with good things.

10 Some were living in gloom and
       darkness,
   prisoners suffering in chains,
11 because they had rebelled against the
       commands of Almighty God
   and had rejected his instructions.
12 They were worn out from hard work;
   they would fall down, and no one
       would help.
13 Then in their trouble they called to the
       LORD,
   and he saved them from their distress.

[d] *Probable text* south; *Hebrew* the Mediterranean Sea *(meaning "west")*.

14 He brought them out of their gloom
and darkness
and broke their chains in pieces.
15 They must thank the LORD for his
constant love,
for the wonderful things he did for
them.
16 He breaks down doors of bronze
and smashes iron bars.

17 Some were fools, suffering because of
their sins
and because of their evil;
18 they couldn't stand the sight of food
and were close to death.
19 Then in their trouble they called to the
LORD,
and he saved them from their distress.
20 He healed them with his command
and saved them from the grave.
21 They must thank the LORD for his
constant love,
for the wonderful things he did for
them.
22 They must thank him with sacrifices,
and with songs of joy must tell all
that he has done.

23 Some sailed over the ocean in ships,
earning their living on the seas.
24 They saw what the LORD can do,
his wonderful acts on the seas.
25 He commanded, and a mighty wind
began to blow
and stirred up the waves.
26 The ships were lifted high in the air
and plunged down into the depths.
In such danger the men lost their
courage;
27 they stumbled and staggered like
drunks—
all their skill was useless.

²⁸ Then in their trouble they called to the
   LORD,
   and he saved them from their distress,
²⁹ He calmed the raging storm,
   and the waves became quiet.
³⁰ They were glad because of the calm,
   and he brought them safe to the port
   they wanted.

And he brought them safe to the port. (107.30)

³¹ They must thank the LORD for his
   constant love,
   for the wonderful things he did for
   them.
³² They must proclaim his greatness in the
   assembly of the people
   and praise him before the council of
   the leaders.

³³ The LORD made rivers dry up
   completely
   and stopped springs from flowing.
³⁴ He made rich soil become a salty
   wasteland
   because of the wickedness of those
   who lived there.

³⁵ He changed deserts into pools of water
and dry land into flowing springs.
³⁶ He let hungry people settle there,
and they built a city to live in.
³⁷ They sowed the fields and planted
grapevines
and reaped an abundant harvest.
³⁸ He blessed his people, and they had
many children;
he kept their herds of cattle from
decreasing.

³⁹ When God's people were defeated and
humiliated
by cruel oppression and suffering,
⁴⁰ he showed contempt for their
oppressors
and made them wander in trackless
deserts.
⁴¹ But he rescued the needy from their
misery
and made their families increase like
flocks.
⁴² The righteous see this and are glad,
but all the wicked are put to silence.

⁴³ May those who are wise think about
these things;
may they consider the LORD's
constant love.

A Prayer for Help against Enemies[f]
(Psalms 57.7-11; 60.5-12)

108 I have complete confidence, O
God!
I will sing and praise you!
Wake up, my soul!
² Wake up, my harp and lyre!
I will wake up the sun.

[f] HEBREW TITLE: *A psalm by David; a song.*

³ I will thank you, O Lord, among the
     nations.
  I will praise you among the peoples.
⁴ Your constant love reaches above the
     heavens;
  your faithfulness touches the skies.

⁵ Show your greatness in the sky, O God,
     and your glory over all the earth.
⁶ Save us by your might; answer my
     prayer,
  so that the people you love may be
     rescued.

⁷ From his sanctuary⁸ God has said,
  "In triumph I will divide Shechem
  and distribute Sukkoth Valley to my
     people.
⁸ Gilead is mine, and Manasseh too;
  Ephraim is my helmet
  and Judah my royal scepter.
⁹ But I will use Moab as my washbowl,
  and I will throw my sandals on
     Edom,
  as a sign that I own it.
  I will shout in triumph over the
     Philistines."

¹⁰ Who, O God, will take me into the
     fortified city?
  Who will lead me to Edom?
¹¹ Have you really rejected us?
  Aren't you going to march out with
     our armies?
¹² Help us against the enemy;
  human help is worthless.
¹³ With God on our side we will win;
  he will defeat our enemies.

⁸ From his sanctuary; or In his holiness.

The Complaint of a Man in Trouble[h]

109 I praise you, God; don't
remain silent!

2 Wicked men and liars have attacked
me.
They tell lies about me,
3   and they say evil things about me,
attacking me for no reason.
4 They oppose me, even though I love
them
and have prayed for them.[i]
5 They pay me back evil for good
and hatred for love.

6 Choose some corrupt judge to try my
enemy,
and let one of his own enemies
accuse him.
7 May he be tried and found guilty;
may even his prayer be considered a
crime!
8 May his life soon be ended;
may another man take his job!
9 May his children become orphans,
and his wife a widow!
10 May his children be homeless beggars;
may they be driven from[j] the ruins
they live in!
11 May his creditors take away all his
property,
and may strangers get everything he
worked for.
12 May no one ever be kind to him
or care for the orphans he leaves
behind.
13 May all his descendants die,
and may his name be forgotten in the
next generation.

[h] HEBREW TITLE: *A psalm by David.* [i] *Probable text* have prayed for
them; *Hebrew unclear.* [j] *One ancient translation* be driven from;
Hebrew seek.

14 May the LORD remember the evil of his
        ancestors
    and never forgive his mother's sins.
15 May the LORD always remember their
        sins,
    but may they themselves be
        completely forgotten!

16 That man never thought of being kind;
        he persecuted and killed
    the poor, the needy, and the helpless.
17 He loved to curse—may he be cursed!
    He hated to give blessings—may no
        one bless him!
18 He cursed as naturally as he dressed
        himself;
    may his own curses soak into his
        body like water
    and into his bones like oil!
19 May they cover him like clothes
    and always be around him like a belt!

20 LORD, punish my enemies in that
        way—
    those who say such evil things against
        me!
21 But my Sovereign LORD, help me as
        you have promised,
    and rescue me because of the
        goodness of your love.
22 I am poor and needy;
    I am hurt to the depths of my heart.
23 Like an evening shadow I am about to
        vanish;
    I am blown away like an insect.
24 My knees are weak from lack of food;
    I am nothing but skin and bones.
25 When people see me, they laugh at me;
    they shake their heads in scorn.

26 Help me, O LORD my God;
    because of your constant love, save
        me!

27 Make my enemies know
    that you are the one who saves me.
28 They may curse me, but you will bless
    me.
    May my persecutors be defeated,*k*
    and may I, your servant, be glad.
29 May my enemies be covered with
    disgrace;
    may they wear their shame like a
    robe.

30 I will give loud thanks to the LORD;
    I will praise him in the assembly of
    the people,
31 because he defends the poor man
    and saves him from those who
    condemn him to death.

The LORD and His Chosen King*l*

110 The LORD said to my lord, the
king,
    "Sit here at my right side
    until I put your enemies under your
    feet."
2 From Zion the LORD will extend your
    royal power.
    "Rule over your enemies," he says.
3 On the day you fight your enemies,
    your people will volunteer.
    Like the dew of early morning
    your young men will come to you on
    the sacred hills.*m*

4 The LORD made a solemn promise and
    will not take it back:
    "You will be a priest forever
    in the priestly order of
    Melchizedek."*n*

k One ancient translation May my persecutors be defeated; *Hebrew*
They persecuted me and were defeated. *l* HEBREW TITLE: *A psalm
by David. m Verse 3 in Hebrew is unclear. n* in the priestly order
of Melchizedek; *or* like Melchizedek; *or* in the line of succession to
Melchizedek.

⁵ The Lord is at your right side;
    when he becomes angry, he will
      defeat kings.
⁶ He will pass judgment on the nations
    and fill the battlefield with corpses;
    he will defeat kings all over the earth.
⁷ The king will drink from the stream by
    the road,
    and strengthened, he will stand
      victorious.

In Praise of the LORD

111 Praise the LORD!

With all my heart I will thank the
    LORD
    in the assembly of his people.
² How wonderful are the things the LORD
    does!
    All who are delighted with them
      want to understand them.
³ All he does is full of honor and majesty;
    his righteousness is eternal.

⁴ The LORD does not let us forget his
    wonderful actions;
    he is kind and merciful.
⁵ He provides food for those who have
    reverence for him;
    he never forgets his covenant.
⁶ He has shown his power to his people
    by giving them the lands of
      foreigners.

⁷ In all he does he is faithful and just;
    all his commands are dependable.
⁸ They last for all time;
    they were given in truth and
      righteousness.

⁹ He set his people free
    and made an eternal covenant with
        them.
    Holy and mighty is he!
¹⁰ The way to become wise is to have
    reverence for the LORD;ᵒ
        he gives sound judgment to all who
            obey his commands.
    He is to be praised forever.

The Happiness of a Good Person

112 Praise the LORD!

Happy is the person who has reverence
    for the LORD,
        who takes pleasure in obeying his
            commands.
² The good man's children will be
    powerful in the land;
        his descendants will be blessed.
³ His family will be wealthy and rich,
    and he will be prosperous forever.

⁴ Light shines in the darkness for good
    men,
        for those who are merciful, kind, and
            just.
⁵ Happy is the person who is generous
    with his loans,
        who runs his business honestly.
⁶ A good person will never fail;
    he will always be remembered.

⁷ He is not afraid of receiving bad news;
    his faith is strong, and he trusts in the
        LORD.
⁸ He is not worried or afraid;
    he is certain to see his enemies
        defeated.

ᵒ The way . . . the LORD; or The most important part of wisdom is
having reverence for the LORD.

8 May all who made them and who trust
 in them
   become,[p] like the idols they have
   made.

9 Trust in the LORD, you people of Israel.
  He helps you and protects you.
10 Trust in the LORD, you priests of God.
  He helps you and protects you.
11 Trust in the LORD, all you that worship
  him.
  He helps you and protects you.

12 The LORD remembers us and will bless
  us;
   he will bless the people of Israel
   and all the priests of God.
13 He will bless everyone who honors
  him,
   the great and the small alike.

14 May the LORD give you children—
  you and your descendants!
15 May you be blessed by the LORD,
  who made heaven and earth!

16 Heaven belongs to the LORD alone,
  but he gave the earth to man.
17 The LORD is not praised by the dead,
  by any who go down to the land of
  silence.[q]
18 But we, the living, will give thanks to
  him
  now and forever.

Praise the LORD!

[p] May all . . . become; or All who made them and who trust in
them will become.   [q] LAND OF SILENCE: *The world of the dead (see
6.5).*

A Man Saved from Death Praises God

116 I love the LORD, because he
hears me;
he listens to my prayers.
2 He listens to me
every time I call to him.
3 The danger of death was all around me;
the horrors of the grave closed in on
me;
I was filled with fear and anxiety.
4 Then I called to the LORD,
"I beg you, LORD, save me!"

5 The LORD is merciful and good;
our God is compassionate.
6 The LORD protects the helpless;
when I was in danger, he saved me.
7 Be confident, my heart,
because the LORD has been good to
me.

8 The LORD saved me from death;
he stopped my tears
and kept me from defeat.
9 And so I walk in the presence of the
LORD
in the world of the living.
10 I kept on believing, even when I said,
"I am completely crushed,"
11 even when I was afraid and said,
"No one can be trusted."

12 What can I offer the LORD
for all his goodness to me?
13 I will bring a wine offering to the
LORD,
to thank him for saving me.
14 In the assembly of all his people
I will give him what I have promised.

15 How painful it is to the LORD
when one of his people dies!

16 I am your servant, LORD;
    I serve you just as my mother did.
You have saved me from death.
17 I will give you a sacrifice of
    thanksgiving
    and offer my prayer to you.
18-19 In the assembly of all your people,
    in the sanctuary of your Temple in
    Jerusalem,
    I will give you what I have promised.

Praise the LORD!

In Praise of the LORD

117 Praise the LORD, all nations!
        Praise him, all peoples!
2 His love for us is strong,
    and his faithfulness is eternal.

Praise the LORD!

A Prayer of Thanks for Victory

118 Give thanks to the LORD,
        because he is good,
    and his love is eternal.
2 Let the people of Israel say,
    "His love is eternal."
3 Let the priests of God say,
    "His love is eternal."
4 Let all who worship him say,
    "His love is eternal."

5 In my distress I called to the LORD;
    he answered me and set me free.
6 The LORD is with me, I will not be
    afraid;
    what can anyone do to me?
7 It is the LORD who helps me,
    and I will see my enemies defeated.

⁸ It is better to trust in the LORD
    than to depend on man.
⁹ It is better to trust in the LORD
    than to depend on human leaders.

¹⁰ Many enemies were around me;
    but I destroyed them by the power of
      the LORD!
¹¹ They were around me on every side;
    but I destroyed them by the power of
      the LORD!
¹² They swarmed around me like bees,
    but they burned out as quickly as a
      brush fire;
    by the power of the LORD I destroyed
      them.
¹³ I was fiercely attacked and was being
      defeated,
    but the LORD helped me.
¹⁴ The LORD makes me powerful and
      strong;
    he has saved me.

¹⁵ Listen to the glad shouts of victory in
      the tents of God's people:
    "The LORD's mighty power has done
      it!
¹⁶   His power has brought us victory—
    his mighty power in battle!"

¹⁷ I will not die; instead, I will live
    and proclaim what the LORD has
      done.
¹⁸ He has punished me severely,
    but he has not let me die.

¹⁹ Open to me the gates of the Temple;
    I will go in and give thanks to the
      LORD!

²⁰ This is the gate of the LORD;
    only the righteous can come in.

²¹ I praise you, LORD, because you heard
me,
because you have given me victory.

²² The stone which the builders rejected as
worthless
turned out to be the most important
of all.
²³ This was done by the LORD;
what a wonderful sight it is!
²⁴ This is the day of the LORD's victory;
let us be happy, let us celebrate!
²⁵ Save us, LORD, save us!
Give us success, O LORD!

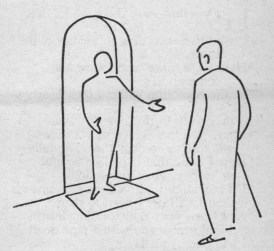

We bless you. (118.26)

²⁶ May God bless the one who comes in
the name of the LORD!
From the Temple of the LORD we
bless you.

²⁷ The LORD is God; he has been good to
us.
With branches in your hands, start the
festival
and march around the altar.

²⁸ You are my God, and I give you
thanks;
I will proclaim your greatness.

²⁹ Give thanks to the LORD, because he is
good,
and his love is eternal.

The Law of the LORD

119 Happy are those whose lives
are faultless,
who live according to the law of the
LORD.
² Happy are those who follow his
commands,
who obey him with all their heart.
³ They never do wrong;
they walk in the LORD's ways.
⁴ LORD, you have given us your laws
and told us to obey them faithfully.
⁵ How I hope that I shall be faithful
in keeping your instructions!
⁶ If I pay attention to all your commands,
then I will not be put to shame.
⁷ As I learn your righteous judgments,
I will praise you with a pure heart.
⁸ I will obey your laws;
never abandon me!

Obedience to the Law of the LORD

⁹ How can a young man keep his life
pure?
By obeying your commands.

¹⁰ With all my heart I try to serve you;
keep me from disobeying your
commandments.
¹¹ I keep your law in my heart,
so that I will not sin against you.
¹² I praise you, O LORD;
teach me your ways.
¹³ I will repeat aloud
all the laws you have given.
¹⁴ I delight in following your commands
more than in having great wealth.
¹⁵ I study your instructions;
I examine your teachings.
¹⁶ I take pleasure in your laws;
your commands I will not forget.

Happiness in the Law of the LORD

¹⁷ Be good to me, your servant,
so that I may live and obey your
teachings.
¹⁸ Open my eyes, so that I may see
the wonderful truths in your law.
¹⁹ I am here on earth for just a little
while;
do not hide your commands from me.
²⁰ My heart aches with longing;
I want to know your judgments at all
times.
²¹ You reprimand the proud;
cursed are those who disobey your
commands.
²² Free me from their insults and scorn,
because I have kept your laws.
²³ The rulers meet and plot against me,
but I will study your teachings.
²⁴ Your instructions give me pleasure;
they are my advisers.

Determination to Obey the Law of the LORD

²⁵ I lie defeated in the dust;
revive me, as you have promised.

²⁶ I confessed all I have done, and you
    answered me;
  teach me your ways.
²⁷ Help me to understand your laws,
    and I will meditate on your
    wonderful teachings.ʳ
²⁸ I am overcome by sorrow;
    strengthen me, as you have promised.
²⁹ Keep me from going the wrong way,
    and in your goodness teach me your
    law.
³⁰ I have chosen to be obedient;
    I have paid attention to your
    judgments.
³¹ I have followed your instructions,
    LORD;
  don't let me be put to shame.
³² I will eagerly obey your commands,
    because you will give me more
    understanding.

A Prayer for Understanding

³³ Teach me, LORD, the meaning of your
    laws,
  and I will obey them at all times.
³⁴ Explain your law to me, and I will obey
    it;
  I will keep it with all my heart.
³⁵ Keep me obedient to your
    commandments,
  because in them I find happiness.
³⁶ Give me the desire to obey your laws
    rather than to get rich.
³⁷ Keep me from paying attention to what
    is worthless;
  be good to me, as you have promised.
³⁸ Keep your promise to me, your
    servant—
  the promise you make to those who
    obey you.

ʳ teachings; *or* deeds.

39 Save me from the insults I fear;
   how wonderful are your judgments!
40 I want to obey your commands;
   give me new life, for you are
      righteous.

Trusting the Law of the LORD

41 Show me how much you love me,
      LORD,
   and save me according to your
      promise.
42 Then I can answer those who insult me
   because I trust in your word.
43 Enable me to speak the truth at all
      times,
   because my hope is in your
      judgments.
44 I will always obey your law,
   forever and ever.
45 I will live in perfect freedom,
   because I try to obey your teachings.
46 I will announce your commands to
      kings
   and I will not be ashamed.
47 I find pleasure in obeying your
      commands,
   because I love them.
48 I respect and love your commandments;
   I will meditate on your instructions.

Confidence in the Law of the LORD

49 Remember your promise to me, your
      servant;
   it has given me hope.
50 Even in my suffering I was comforted
   because your promise gave me life.
51 The proud are always scornful of me,
   but I have not departed from your
      law.

⁵² I remember your judgments of long ago,
and they bring me comfort, O LORD.
⁵³ When I see the wicked breaking your
law,
I am filled with anger.
⁵⁴ During my brief earthly life
I compose songs about your
commands.
⁵⁵ In the night I remember you, LORD,
and I think about your law.
⁵⁶ I find my happiness
in obeying your commands.

Devotion to the Law of the LORD

⁵⁷ You are all I want, O LORD;
I promise to obey your laws.
⁵⁸ I ask you with all my heart
to have mercy on me, as you have
promised!
⁵⁹ I have considered my conduct,
and I promise to follow your
instructions.
⁶⁰ Without delay I hurry
to obey your commands.
⁶¹ The wicked have laid a trap for me,
but I do not forget your law.
⁶² In the middle of the night I wake up
to praise you for your righteous
judgments.
⁶³ I am a friend of all who serve you,
of all who obey your laws.
⁶⁴ LORD, the earth is full of your constant
love;
teach me your commandments.

The Value of the Law of the LORD

⁶⁵ You have kept your promise, LORD,
and you are good to me, your
servant.

[66] Give me wisdom and knowledge,
because I trust in your commands.
[67] Before you punished me, I used to go
wrong,
but now I obey your word.
[68] How good you are—how kind!
Teach me your commands.
[69] Proud men have told lies about me,
but with all my heart I obey your
instructions.
[70] These men have no understanding,
but I find pleasure in your law.
[71] My punishment was good for me,
because it made me learn your
commands.
[72] The law that you gave means more to
me
than all the money in the world.

The Justice of the Law of the LORD

[73] You created me, and you keep me safe;
give me understanding, so that I may
learn your laws.
[74] Those who have reverence for you will
be glad when they see me,
because I trust in your promise.
[75] I know that your judgments are
righteous, LORD,
and that you punished me because
you are faithful.
[76] Let your constant love comfort me,
as you have promised me, your
servant.
[77] Have mercy on me, and I will live
because I take pleasure in your law.
[78] May the proud be ashamed for falsely
accusing me;
as for me, I will meditate on your
instructions.
[79] May those who have reverence for you
come to me—
all those who know your commands.

⁸⁰ May I perfectly obey your
commandments
and be spared the shame of defeat.

A Prayer for Deliverance

⁸¹ I am worn out, LORD, waiting for you
to save me;
I place my trust in your word.
⁸² My eyes are tired from watching for
what you promised,
while I ask, "When will you help
me?"
⁸³ I am as useless as a discarded wineskin;
yet I have not forgotten your
commands.
⁸⁴ How much longer must I wait?
When will you punish those who
persecute me?
⁸⁵ Proud men, who do not obey your law,
have dug pits to trap me.
⁸⁶ Your commandments are all
trustworthy;
men persecute me with lies—help me!
⁸⁷ They have almost succeeded in killing
me,
but I have not neglected your
commands.
⁸⁸ Because of your constant love be good
to me,
so that I may obey your laws.

Faith in the Law of the LORD

⁸⁹ Your word, O LORD, will last forever;
it is eternal in heaven.
⁹⁰ Your faithfulness endures through all
the ages;
you have set the earth in place, and it
remains.
⁹¹ All things remain to this day because of
your command,
because they are all your servants.

⁹² If your law had not been the source of
　　my joy,
　　I would have died from my sufferings.
⁹³ I will never neglect your instructions,
　　because by them you have kept me
　　alive.
⁹⁴ I am yours—save me!
　　I have tried to obey your commands.
⁹⁵ Wicked men are waiting to kill me,
　　but I will meditate on your laws.
⁹⁶ I have learned that everything has
　　limits;
　　but your commandment is perfect.

Love for the Law of the LORD

⁹⁷ How I love your law!
　　I think about it all day long.
⁹⁸ Your commandment is with me all the
　　time
　　and makes me wiser than my
　　enemies.
⁹⁹ I understand more than all my teachers,
　　because I meditate on your
　　instructions.
¹⁰⁰ I have greater wisdom than old men,
　　because I obey your commands.
¹⁰¹ I have avoided all evil conduct,
　　because I want to obey your word.
¹⁰² I have not neglected your instructions,
　　because you yourself are my teacher.
¹⁰³ How sweet is the taste of your
　　instructions—
　　sweeter even than honey!
¹⁰⁴ I gain wisdom from your laws,
　　and so I hate all bad conduct.

Light from the Law of the LORD

¹⁰⁵ Your word is a lamp to guide me
　　and a light for my path.
¹⁰⁶ I will keep my solemn promise
　　to obey your just instructions.

A light for my path. (119.105)

¹⁰⁷ My sufferings, LORD, are terrible
indeed;
keep me alive, as you have promised.
¹⁰⁸ Accept my prayer of thanks, O LORD,
and teach me your commands.
¹⁰⁹ I am always ready to risk my life;
Iˢ have not forgotten your law.
¹¹⁰ Wicked men lay a trap for me,
but I have not disobeyed your
commands.
¹¹¹ Your commandments are my eternal
possession;
they are the joy of my heart.
¹¹² I have decided to obey your laws
until the day I die.

ˢ I am always ready to risk my life; I; *or* My life is in constant
danger, but I.

Safety in the Law of the LORD

113 I hate those who are not completely
    loyal to you,
    but I love your law.
114 You are my defender and protector;
    I put my hope in your promise.
115 Go away from me, you sinful people.
    I will obey the commands of my God.
116 Give me strength, as you promised, and
    I shall live;
    don't let me be disappointed in my
    hope!
117 Hold me, and I will be safe,
    and I will always pay attention to
    your commands.
118 You reject everyone who disobeys your
    laws;
    their deceitful schemes are useless.
119 You treat all the wicked like rubbish,
    and so I love your instructions.
120 Because of you I am afraid;
    I am filled with fear because of your
    judgments.

Obedience to the Law of the LORD

121 I have done what is right and good;
    don't abandon me to my enemies!
122 Promise that you will help your
    servant;
    don't let arrogant men oppress me!
123 My eyes are tired from watching for
    your saving help,
    for the deliverance you promised.
124 Treat me according to your constant
    love,
    and teach me your commands.
125 I am your servant; give me
    understanding,
    so that I may know your teachings.

126 LORD, it is time for you to act,
   because people are disobeying your
      law.
127 I love your commands more than gold,
   more than the finest gold.
128 And so I follow all your instructions;[t]
   I hate all wrong ways.

Desire to Obey the Law of the LORD

129 Your teachings are wonderful;
   I obey them with all my heart.
130 The explanation of your teachings gives
      light
   and brings wisdom to the ignorant.
131 In my desire for your commands
   I pant with open mouth.
132 Turn to me and have mercy on me
   as you do on all those who love you.
133 As you have promised, keep me from
      falling;
   don't let me be overcome by evil.
134 Save me from those who oppress me,
   so that I may obey your commands.
135 Bless me with your presence
   and teach me your laws.
136 My tears pour down like a river,
   because people do not obey your law.

The Justice of the Law of the LORD

137 You are righteous, LORD,
   and your laws are just.
138 The rules that you have given
   are completely fair and right.
139 My anger burns in me like a fire,
   because my enemies disregard your
      commands.

[t] *Some ancient translations* all your instructions; *Hebrew unclear.*

140 How certain your promise is!
   How I love it!
141 I am unimportant and despised,
   but I do not neglect your teachings.
142 Your righteousness will last forever,
   and your law is always true.
143 I am filled with trouble and anxiety,
   but your commandments bring me
   joy.
144 Your instructions are always just;
   give me understanding, and I shall
   live.

A Prayer for Deliverance

145 With all my heart I call to you;
   answer me, LORD, and I will obey
   your commands!
146 I call to you;
   save me, and I will keep your laws.
147 Before sunrise I call to you for help;
   I place my hope in your promise.
148 All night long I lie awake,
   to meditate on your instructions.
149 Because your love is constant, hear me,
   O LORD;
   show your mercy, and preserve my
   life!
150 My cruel persecutors are coming closer,
   people who never keep your law.
151 But you are near to me, LORD,
   and all your commands are
   permanent.
152 Long ago I learned about your
   instructions;
   you made them to last forever.

A Plea for Help

153 Look at my suffering, and save me,
   because I have not neglected your
   law.

154 Defend my cause, and set me free;
    save me, as you have promised.
155 The wicked will not be saved,
    for they do not obey your laws.
156 But your compassion, LORD, is great;
    show your mercy and save me!
157 I have many enemies and oppressors,
    but I do not fail to obey your laws.
158 When I look at those traitors, I am
       filled with disgust,
    because they do not keep your
       commands.
159 See how I love your instructions, LORD.
    Your love never changes, so save me!
160 The heart of your law is truth,
    and all your righteous judgments are
       eternal.

Dedication to the Law of the LORD

161 Powerful men attack me unjustly,
    but I respect your law.
162 How happy I am because of your
       promises—
    as happy as someone who finds rich
       treasure.
163 I hate and detest all lies,
    but I love your law.
164 Seven times each day I thank you
    for your righteous judgments.
165 Those who love your law have perfect
       security,
    and there is nothing that can make
       them fall.
166 I wait for you to save me, LORD,
    and I do what you command.
167 I obey your teachings;
    I love them with all my heart.
168 I obey your commands and your
       instructions;
    you see everything I do.

A Prayer for Help

169 Let my cry for help reach you, LORD!
    Give me understanding, as you have
        promised
170 Listen to my prayer,
    and save me according to your
        promise!
171 I will always praise you,
    because you teach me your laws.
172 I will sing about your law,
    because your commands are just.
173 Always be ready to help me,
    because I follow your commands.
174 How I long for your saving help, O
        LORD!
    I find happiness in your law.
175 Give me life, so that I may praise you;
    may your instructions help me.
176 I wander about like a lost sheep;
    so come and look for me, your
        servant,
    because I have not neglected your
        laws.

A Prayer for Help

120 When I was in trouble, I called
        to the LORD,
    and he answered me.
2 Save me, LORD,
    from liars and deceivers.

3 You liars, what will God do to you?
    How will he punish you?
4 With a soldier's sharp arrows,
    with red-hot coals!

5 Living among you is as bad as living in
        Meshech
    or among the people of Kedar.u

---

u MESHECH . . . KEDAR: *Two distant regions, whose people were
regarded as savages.*

⁶ I have lived too long
    with people who hate peace!
⁷ When I speak of peace,
    they are for war.

The LORD Our Protector

121 I look to the mountains;
        where will my help come
        from?
² My help will come from the LORD,
    who made heaven and earth.

³ He will not let you fall;
    your protector is always awake.

⁴ The protector of Israel
    never dozes or sleeps.
⁵ The LORD will guard you;
    he is by your side to protect you.
⁶ The sun will not hurt you during the
    day,
    nor the moon during the night.

⁷ The LORD will protect you from all
    danger;
    he will keep you safe.
⁸ He will protect you as you come and go
    now and forever.

In Praise of Jerusalem ᵛ

122 I was glad when they said to
        me,
    "Let us go to the LORD's house."
² And now we are here,
    standing inside the gates of
        Jerusalem!

³ Jerusalem is a city restored
    in beautiful order and harmony.

ᵛ HEBREW TITLE: *By David.*

⁴ This is where the tribes come,
    the tribes of Israel,
 to give thanks to the LORD
    according to his command.
⁵ Here the kings of Israel
    sat to judge their people.

⁶ Pray for the peace of Jerusalem:
    "May those who love you prosper.
⁷   May there be peace inside your walls
    and safety in your palaces."
⁸ For the sake of my relatives and friends
    I say to Jerusalem, "Peace be with
    you!"
⁹ For the sake of the house of the LORD
    our God
    I pray for your prosperity.

A Prayer for Mercy

123   LORD, I look up to you,
          up to heaven, where you
          rule.
² As a servant depends on his master,
    as a maid depends on her mistress,
so we will keep looking to you, O LORD
    our God,
    until you have mercy on us.

³ Be merciful to us, LORD, be merciful;
    we have been treated with so much
    contempt.
⁴ We have been mocked too long by the
    rich
    and scorned by proud oppressors.

God the Protector of His People ʷ

124   What if the LORD had not been
          on our side?
Answer, O Israel!

ʷ HEBREW TITLE: *By David.*

2 "If the Lord had not been on our side
    when our enemies attacked us,
3 then they would have swallowed us
        alive
    in their furious anger against us;
4 then the flood would have carried us
        away,
    the water would have covered us,
5   the raging torrent would have
        drowned us."

6 Let us thank the Lord,
    who has not let our enemies destroy
        us.
7 We have escaped like a bird from a
        hunter's trap;
    the trap is broken, and we are free!
8 Our help comes from the Lord,
    who made heaven and earth.

The Security of God's People

125   Those who trust in the Lord
            are like Mount Zion,
    which can never be shaken, never be
        moved.
2 As the mountains surround Jerusalem,
    so the Lord surrounds his people,
    now and forever.

3 The wicked will not always rule over
        the land of the righteous;
    if they did, the righteous themselves
        might do evil.
4 Lord, do good to those who are good,
    to those who obey your commands.
5 But when you punish the wicked,
    punish also those who abandon your
        ways.

Peace be with Israel!

A Prayer for Deliverance

126 When the LORD brought us
back to Jerusalem,[x]
it was like a dream!
2 How we laughed, how we sang for joy!
Then the other nations said about us,
"The LORD did great things for
them."
3 Indeed he did great things for us;
how happy we were!

4 LORD, make us prosperous again,[y]
just as the rain brings water back to
dry riverbeds.

Gather the harvest with joy! (126.5)

[x] brought us back to Jerusalem; *or* made Jerusalem prosperous
again.   [y] make us prosperous again; *or* take us back to our land.

⁵ Let those who wept as they planted
    their crops,
    gather the harvest with joy!

⁶ Those who wept as they went out
    carrying the seed
    will come back singing for joy,
    as they bring in the harvest.

In Praise of God's Goodness ²

127 If the LORD does not build the
    house,
    the work of the builders is useless;
if the LORD does not protect the city,
    it does no good for the sentries to
    stand guard.
² It is useless to work so hard for a
    living,
    getting up early and going to bed late.
For the LORD provides for those he
    loves,
    while they are asleep.

³ Children are a gift from the LORD;
    they are a real blessing.
⁴ The sons a man has when he is young
    are like arrows in a soldier's hand.
⁵ Happy is the man who has many such
    arrows.
He will never be defeated
    when he meets his enemies in the
    place of judgment.

The Reward of Obedience to the LORD

128 Happy are those who obey the
    LORD,
    who live by his commands.

² HEBREW TITLE: *By Solomon.*

2 Your work will provide for your needs;
  you will be happy and prosperous.
3 Your wife will be like a fruitful vine in
    your home,
    and your sons will be like young
      olive trees around your table.
4 A man who obeys the LORD
    will surely be blessed like this.

5 May the LORD bless you from Zion!
    May you see Jerusalem prosper
    all the days of your life!
6 May you live to see your grandchildren!

Peace be with Israel!

A Prayer against Israel's Enemies

129 Israel, tell us how your
      enemies have persecuted
      you
    ever since you were young.

2 "Ever since I was young,
    my enemies have persecuted me
      cruelly,
    but they have not overcome me.
3 They cut deep wounds in my back
    and made it like a plowed field.
4 But the LORD, the righteous one,
    has freed me from slavery."

5 May everyone who hates Zion
    be defeated and driven back.
6 May they all be like grass growing on
      the housetops,
    which dries up before it can grow;
7   no one gathers it up
    or carries it away in bundles.
8 No one who passes by will say,
    "May the LORD bless you!
    We bless you in the name of the
      LORD."

A Prayer for Help

130 From the depths of my despair
I call to you, LORD.
2 Hear my cry, O Lord;
listen to my call for help!
3 If you kept a record of our sins,
who could escape being condemned?
4 But you forgive us,
so that we should reverently obey
you.

5 I wait eagerly for the LORD's help,
and in his word I trust.
6 I wait for the Lord
more eagerly than watchmen wait for
the dawn—
than watchmen wait for the dawn.

7 Israel, trust in the LORD,
because his love is constant
and he is always willing to save.
8 He will save his people Israel
from all their sins.

A Prayer of Humble Trust[z]

131 LORD, I have given up my
pride
and turned away from my arrogance.
I am not concerned with great matters
or with subjects too difficult for me.
2 Instead, I am content and at peace.
As a child lies quietly in its mother's
arms,
so my heart is quiet within me.
3 Israel, trust in the LORD
now and forever!

[z] HEBREW TITLE: *By David.*

In Praise of the Temple

132   LORD, do not forget David
and all the hardships he
endured.
2 Remember, LORD, what he promised,
the vow he made to you, the Mighty
God of Jacob:
3 "I will not go home or go to bed;
4   I will not rest or sleep,
5   until I provide a place for the LORD,
a home for the Mighty God of
Jacob."

6 In Bethlehem we heard about the
Covenant Box,
and we found it in the fields of
Jearim.
7 We said, "Let us go to the LORD's
house;
let us worship before his throne."

8 Come to the Temple, LORD, with the
Covenant Box,
the symbol of your power,
and stay here forever.
9 May your priests do always what is
right;
may your people shout for joy!

10 You made a promise to your servant
David;
do not reject your chosen king, LORD.
11 You made a solemn promise to
David—
a promise you will not take back:
"I will make one of your sons king,
and he will rule after you.
12 If your sons are true to my covenant
and to the commands I give them,
their sons, also, will succeed you for
all time as kings."

¹³ The LORD has chosen Zion;
  he wants to make it his home:
¹⁴ "This is where I will live forever;
  this is where I want to rule.
¹⁵ I will richly provide Zion with all she
    needs;
  I will satisfy her poor with food.
¹⁶ I will bless her priests in all they do,
  and her people will sing and shout
    for joy.
¹⁷ Here I will make one of David's
    descendants a great king;
  here I will preserve the rule of my
    chosen king.
¹⁸ I will cover his enemies with shame,
  but his kingdom will prosper and
    flourish."

In Praise of Brotherly Loveᵃ

133 How wonderful it is, how
      pleasant,
  for God's people to live together in
    harmony!
² It is like the precious anointing oil
  running down from Aaron's head and
    beard,
  down to the collar of his robes.
³ It is like the dew on Mount Hermon,
  falling on the hills of Zion.
  That is where the LORD has promised
    his blessing—
  life that never ends.

A Call to Praise God

134 Come, praise the LORD,
      all his servants,
  all who serve in his Temple at night.

ᵃ HEBREW TITLE: *By David.*

2 Raise your hands in prayer in the
 Temple,
 and praise the LORD!

3 May the LORD, who made heaven and
 earth,
 bless you from Zion!

A Hymn of Praise

135 Praise the LORD!

Praise his name, you servants of the
 LORD,
2   who stand in the LORD's house,
 in the Temple of our God.
3 Praise the LORD, because he is good;
 sing praises to his name, because he
 is kind.*b*
4 He chose Jacob for himself,
 the people of Israel for his own.

5 I know that our LORD is great,
 greater than all the gods.
6 He does whatever he wishes
 in heaven and on earth,
 in the seas and in the depths below.
7 He brings storm clouds from the ends
 of the earth;
 he makes lightning for the storms,
 and he brings out the wind from his
 storeroom.

8 In Egypt he killed all the first-born
 of men and animals alike.
9 There he performed miracles and
 wonders
 to punish the king and all his
 officials.
10 He destroyed many nations
 and killed powerful kings:

b he is kind; *or* it is pleasant to do so.

¹¹ Sihon, king of the Amorites,
    Og, king of Bashan,
    and all the kings in Canaan.
¹² He gave their lands to his people;
    he gave them to Israel.

¹³ LORD, you will always be proclaimed as
        God;
    all generations will remember you.
¹⁴ The LORD will defend his people;
    he will take pity on his servants.

¹⁵ The gods of the nations are made of
        silver and gold;
    they are formed by human hands.
¹⁶ They have mouths, but cannot speak,
    and eyes, but cannot see.
¹⁷ They have ears, but cannot hear;
    they are not even able to breathe.
¹⁸ May all who made them and who trust
        in them
    become *c* like the idols they have
        made!

¹⁹ Praise the LORD, people of Israel;
    praise him, you priests of God!
²⁰ Praise the LORD, you Levites;
    praise him, all you that worship him!
²¹ Praise the LORD in Zion,
    in Jerusalem, his home.

    Praise the LORD!

A Hymn of Thanksgiving

136 Give thanks to the LORD,
        because he is good;
    his love is eternal.
² Give thanks to the greatest of all gods;
    his love is eternal.

---

c May all . . . become; *or* All who made them and who trust in
them will become.

³ Give thanks to the mightiest of all
     lords;
  his love is eternal.

⁴ He alone performs great miracles;
  his love is eternal.
⁵ By his wisdom he made the heavens;
  his love is eternal;
⁶ he built the earth on the deep waters;
  his love is eternal.
⁷ He made the sun and the moon;
  his love is eternal;
⁸ the sun to rule over the day;
  his love is eternal;
⁹ the moon and the stars to rule over the
     night;
  his love is eternal.

¹⁰ He killed the first-born sons of the
     Egyptians;
   his love is eternal.
¹¹ He led the people of Israel out of
     Egypt;
   his love is eternal;
¹² with his strong hand, his powerful arm;
   his love is eternal.
¹³ He divided the Red Sea;
   his love is eternal;
¹⁴ he led his people through it;
   his love is eternal;
¹⁵ but he drowned the king of Egypt and
     his army;
   his love is eternal.

¹⁶ He led his people through the desert;
   his love is eternal.
¹⁷ He killed powerful kings;
   his love is eternal;
¹⁸ he killed famous kings;
   his love is eternal;
¹⁹ Sihon, king of the Amorites;
   his love is eternal;

²⁰ and Og, king of Bashan;
　　his love is eternal.
²¹ He gave their lands to his people;
　　his love is eternal;
²² he gave them to Israel, his servant;
　　his love is eternal.

²³ He did not forget us when we were
　　defeated;
　　his love is eternal;
²⁴ he freed us from our enemies;
　　his love is eternal.
²⁵ He gives food to every living creature;
　　his love is eternal.

²⁶ Give thanks to the God of heaven;
　　his love is eternal.

A Lament of Israelites in Exile

137 By the rivers of Babylon we
　　　　sat down;
　　there we wept when we remembered
　　Zion.
² On the willows near by
　　we hung up our harps.
³ Those who captured us told us to sing;
　　they told us to entertain them:
　　"Sing us a song about Zion."

⁴ How can we sing a song to the LORD
　　in a foreign land?
⁵ May I never be able to play the harp
　　again
　　if I forget you, Jerusalem!
⁶ May I never be able to sing again
　　if I do not remember you,
　　if I do not think of you as my greatest
　　joy!

⁷ Remember, LORD, what the Edomites
    did
  the day Jerusalem was captured.
Remember how they kept saying,
  "Tear it down to the ground!"

⁸ Babylon, you will be destroyed.
Happy is the man who pays you back
    for what you have done to us—
  ⁹ who takes your babies
    and smashes them against a rock.

A Prayer of Thanksgiving[d]

138   I thank you, LORD, with all my
          heart;
    I sing praise to you before the gods.
² I face your holy Temple,
    bow down, and praise your name
  because of your constant love and
      faithfulness,
      because you have shown that your
        name and your commands are
        supreme.[e]
³ You answered me when I called to you;
    with your strength you strengthened
      me.

⁴ All the kings in the world will praise
      you, LORD,
    because they have heard your
      promises.
⁵ They will sing about what you have
      done
    and about your great glory.
⁶ Even though you are so high above,
    you care for the lowly,
    and the proud cannot hide from you.

[d] HEBREW TITLE: *By David.*   [e] *Probable text* your name and your
commands are supreme; *Hebrew* your command is greater than all
your name.

7 When I am surrounded by troubles,
  you keep me safe.
You oppose my angry enemies
  and save me by your power.
8 You will do everything you have
    promised;
  LORD, your love is eternal.
  Complete the work that you have
    begun.

God's Complete Knowledge and Care *f*

139 LORD, you have examined me
     and you know me.
2 You know everything I do;
  from far away you understand all my
    thoughts.
3 You see me, whether I am working or
    resting;
  you know all my actions.
4 Even before I speak,
  you already know what I will say.
5 You are all around me on every side;
  you protect me with your power.
6 Your knowledge of me is too deep;
  it is beyond my understanding.

7 Where could I go to escape from you?
  Where could I get away from your
    presence?
8 If I went up to heaven, you would be
    there;
  if I lay down in the world of the
    dead, you would be there.
9 If I flew away beyond the east
  or lived in the farthest place in the
    west,
10 you would be there to lead me,
  you would be there to help me.

f HEBREW TITLE: *A psalm by David.*

¹¹ I could ask the darkness to hide me
>   or the light around me to turn into
>   night,
¹² but even darkness is not dark for you,
>   and the night is as bright as the day.
>   Darkness and light are the same to
>   you.

¹³ You created every part of me;
>   you put me together in my mother's
>   womb.
¹⁴ I praise you because you are to be
>   feared;
>   all you do is strange and wonderful.
>   I know it with all my heart.
¹⁵ When my bones were being formed,
>   carefully put together in my mother's
>   womb,
>   when I was growing there in secret,
>   you knew that I was there—
¹⁶   you saw me before I was born.
>   The days allotted to me
>   had all been recorded in your book,
>   before any of them ever began.
¹⁷ O God, how difficult I find your
>   thoughts;^g
>   how many of them there are!
¹⁸ If I counted them, they would be more
>   than the grains of sand.
>   When I awake, I am still with you.

¹⁹ O God, how I wish you would kill the
>   wicked!
>   How I wish violent men would leave
>   me alone!
²⁰ They say wicked things about you;
>   they speak evil things against your
>   name.^h

---

^g how difficult I find your thoughts; *or* how precious are your
thoughts to me.   ^h *Probable text* they speak . . . name; *Hebrew
unclear.*

²¹ O LORD, how I hate those who hate
    you!
    How I despise those who rebel
        against you!
²² I hate them with a total hatred;
    I regard them as my enemies.

²³ Examine me, O God, and know my
        mind;
    test me, and discover my thoughts.
²⁴ Find out if there is any evil in me
    and guide me in the everlasting way.*ⁱ*

A Prayer for Protection *ʲ*

140 Save me, LORD, from evil men;
        keep me safe from violent
        men.
² They are always plotting evil,
    always stirring up quarrels.
³ Their tongues are like deadly snakes;
    their words are like a cobra's poison.

⁴ Protect me, LORD, from the power of
        the wicked;
    keep me safe from violent men
    who plot my downfall.
⁵ Proud men have set a trap for me;
    they have laid their snares,
    and along the path they have set
        traps to catch me.

⁶ I say to the LORD, "You are my God."
    Hear my cry for help, LORD!
⁷ My Sovereign LORD, my strong
        defender,
    you have protected me in battle.
⁸ LORD, don't give the wicked what they
        want;
    don't let their plots succeed.

ⁱ the everlasting way; *or* the ways of my ancestors.   *ʲ* HEBREW
TITLE: *A psalm by David.*

9 Don't let my enemies be victorious;[k]
    make their threats against me fall
      back on them.
10 May red-hot coals fall on them;
    may they be thrown into a pit and
      never get out.
11 May those who accuse others falsely
      not succeed;
    may evil overtake violent men and
      destroy them.

12 LORD, I know that you defend the cause
      of the poor
    and the rights of the needy.
13 The righteous will praise you indeed;
    they will live in your presence.

An Evening Prayer[l]

141   I call to you, LORD; help me
           now!
    Listen to me when I call to you.
2 Receive my prayer as incense,
    my uplifted hands as an evening
      sacrifice.

3 LORD, place a guard at my mouth,
    a sentry at the door of my lips.
4 Keep me from wanting to do wrong
    and from joining evil men in their
      wickedness.
May I never take part in their feasts.

5 A good man may punish me and rebuke
      me in kindness,
    but I will never accept honor from
      evil men,
    because I am always praying against
      their evil deeds.

---

[k] *Probable text* Don't let my enemies be victorious; *Hebrew unclear.*
[l] HEBREW TITLE: *A psalm by David.*

⁶ When their rulers are thrown down
    from rocky cliffs,
    the people will admit that my words
      were true.
⁷ Like wood that is split and chopped
    into bits,
    so their bones are scattered at the
      edge of the grave.ᵐ

⁸ But I keep trusting in you, my
    Sovereign LORD.
    I seek your protection;
    don't let me die!
⁹ Protect me from the traps they have set
    for me,
    from the snares of those evildoers.
¹⁰ May the wicked fall into their own
    traps
    while I go by unharmed.

A Prayer for Helpⁿ

142   I call to the LORD for help;
            I plead with him.
² I bring him all my complaints;
    I tell him all my troubles.
³ When I am ready to give up,
    he knows what I should do.
In the path where I walk,
    my enemies have hidden a trap for
      me.
⁴ When I look beside me,
    I see that there is no one to help me,
    no one to protect me.
No one cares for me.

⁵ LORD, I cry to you for help;
    you, LORD, are my protector;
    you are all I want in this life.

ᵐ *Verses 5–7 in Hebrew are unclear.*   ⁿ HEBREW TITLE: *A poem by David, when he was in the cave; a prayer.*

⁶ Listen to my cry for help,
    for I am sunk in despair.
Save me from my enemies;
    they are too strong for me.
⁷ Set me free from my distress;*
    then in the assembly of your people I
        will praise you
    because of your goodness to me.

A Prayer for Help*

143 LORD, hear my prayer!
    In your righteousness listen to
        my plea;
    answer me in your faithfulness!
² Don't put me, your servant, on trial;
    no one is innocent in your sight.

³ My enemy has hunted me down
    and completely defeated me.
He has put me in a dark prison,
    and I am like those who died long
        ago.
⁴ So I am ready to give up;
    I am in deep despair.

⁵ I remember the days gone by;
    I think about all that you have done,
    I bring to mind all your deeds.
⁶ I lift up my hands to you in prayer;
    like dry ground my soul is thirsty for
        you.

⁷ Answer me now, LORD!
    I have lost all hope.
Don't hide yourself from me,
    or I will be among those who go
        down to the world of the dead.
⁸ Remind me each morning of your
        constant love,
    for I put my trust in you.

---

*distress; *or* prison.   *HEBREW TITLE: *A psalm by David.*

My prayers go up to you;
   show me the way I should go.

9 I go to you for protection, LORD;
   rescue me from my enemies.
10 You are my God;
   teach me to do your will.
Be good to me, and guide me on a safe
   path.

11 Rescue me, LORD, as you have
    promised;
   in your goodness save me from my
    troubles!
12 Because of your love for me, kill my
    enemies
   and destroy all my oppressors,
   for I am your servant.

A King Thanks God for Victory *q*

144 Praise the LORD, my protector!
   He trains me for battle
and prepares me for war.
2 He is my protector and defender,
   my shelter and savior,
   in whom I trust for safety.
He subdues the nations under me.

3 LORD, what is man, that you notice
    him;
   mere man, that you pay attention to
    him?
4 He is like a puff of wind;
   his days are like a passing shadow.

5 O LORD, tear the sky open and come
    down;
   touch the mountains, and they will
    pour out smoke.

q HEBREW TITLE: *By David.*

⁶ Send flashes of lightning and scatter
     your enemies;
    shoot your arrows and send them
     running.
⁷ Reach down from above,
    pull me out of the deep water, and
     rescue me;
    save me from the power of foreigners,
⁸   who never tell the truth
    and lie even under oath.

⁹ I will sing you a new song, O God;
    I will play the harp and sing to you.
¹⁰ You give victory to kings
    and rescue your servant David.
¹¹ Save me from my cruel enemies;
    rescue me from the power of
     foreigners,
    who never tell the truth
    and lie even under oath.

¹² May our sons in their youth
    be like plants that grow up strong.
  May our daughters be like stately
     columns
    which adorn the corners of a palace.
¹³ May our barns be filled
    with crops of every kind.
  May the sheep in our fields
    bear young by the tens of thousands.
¹⁴ May our cattle reproduce plentifully
    without miscarriage or loss.
  May there be no cries of distress in our
     streets.

¹⁵ Happy is the nation of whom this is
     true;
    happy are the people whose God is
    the LORD!

A Hymn of Praise[r]

145
I will proclaim your greatness,
my God and king;
I will thank you forever and ever.

2 Every day I will thank you;
I will praise you forever and ever.

3 The LORD is great and is to be highly
praised;
his greatness is beyond
understanding.

4 What you have done will be praised
from one generation to the next;
they will proclaim your mighty acts.

5 They will speak of your glory and
majesty,
and I will meditate on your
wonderful deeds.

6 People will speak of your mighty deeds,
and I will proclaim your greatness.

7 They will tell about all your goodness
and sing about your kindness.

8 The LORD is loving and merciful,
slow to become angry and full of
constant love.

9 He is good to everyone
and has compassion on all he made.

10 All your creatures, LORD, will praise
you,
and all your people will give you
thanks.

11 They will speak of the glory of your
royal power
and tell of your might,

12 so that everyone will know your mighty
deeds
and the glorious majesty of your
kingdom.

13 Your rule is eternal,
and you are king forever.

[r] HEBREW TITLE: *A song of praise by David.*

The LORD is faithful to his promises;
   he is merciful in all his acts.
14 He helps those who are in trouble;
   he lifts those who have fallen.

15 All living things look hopefully to you,
   and you give them food when they
     need it.
16 You give them enough
   and satisfy the needs of all.

17 The LORD is righteous in all he does,
   merciful in all his acts.
18 He is near to those who call to him,
   who call to him with sincerity.
19 He supplies the needs of those who
    honor him;
   he hears their cries and saves them.
20 He protects everyone who loves him,
   but he will destroy the wicked.

21 I will always praise the LORD;
   let all his creatures praise his holy
    name forever.

In Praise of God the Savior

146 Praise the LORD!
    Praise the LORD, my soul!
2 I will praise him as long as I live;
   I will sing to my God all my life.

3 Don't put your trust in human leaders;
   no human being can save you.
4 When they die, they return to the dust;
   on that day all their plans come to an
    end.

5 Happy is the man who has the God of
    Jacob to help him
   and who depends on the LORD his
    God,

⁶　the Creator of heaven, earth, and sea,
　　and all that is in them.
　He always keeps his promises;
⁷　he judges in favor of the oppressed
　　and gives food to the hungry.

　The LORD sets prisoners free
⁸　and gives sight to the blind.
　He lifts those who have fallen;
　　he loves his righteous people.
⁹ He protects the strangers who live in
　　　our land;
　　he helps widows and orphans,
　　but takes the wicked to their ruin.

And gives food to the hungry. (146.7)

¹⁰ The LORD is king forever.
      Your God, O Zion, will reign for all
         time.

Praise the LORD!

In Praise of God the Almighty

147   Praise the LORD!

   It is good to sing praise to our God;
      it is pleasant and right to praise him.
² The LORD is restoring Jerusalem;
      he is bringing back the exiles.
³ He heals the broken-hearted
      and bandages their wounds.

⁴ He has decided the number of the stars
      and calls each one by name.
⁵ Great and mighty is our Lord;
      his wisdom cannot be measured.
⁶ He raises the humble,
      but crushes the wicked to the ground.

⁷ Sing hymns of praise to the LORD;
      play music on the harp to our God.
⁸ He spreads clouds over the sky;
      he provides rain for the earth
      and makes grass grow on the hills.
⁹ He gives animals their food
      and feeds the young ravens when
         they call.

¹⁰ His pleasure is not in strong horses,
      nor his delight in brave soldiers;
¹¹ but he takes pleasure in those who
         honor him,
      in those who trust in his constant
         love.

¹² Praise the LORD, O Jerusalem!
      Praise your God, O Zion!

¹³ He keeps your gates strong;
   he blesses your people.
¹⁴ He keeps your borders safe
   and satisfies you with the finest
      wheat.

¹⁵ He gives a command to the earth,
   and what he says is quickly done.
¹⁶ He spreads snow like a blanket
   and scatters frost like dust.
¹⁷ He sends hail like gravel;
   no one can endure the cold he sends!
¹⁸ Then he gives a command, and the ice
      melts;
   he sends the wind, and the water
      flows.

¹⁹ He gives his message to his people,
   his instructions and laws to Israel.
²⁰ He has not done this for other nations;
   they do not know his laws.

Praise the LORD!

A Call for the Universe to Praise God

148 Praise the LORD!

Praise the LORD from heaven,
   you that live in the heights above.
² Praise him, all his angels,
   all his heavenly armies.

³ Praise him, sun and moon;
   praise him, shining stars.
⁴ Praise him, highest heavens,
   and the waters above the sky.⁵

⁵ Let them all praise the name of the
      LORD!
   He commanded, and they were created;

⁵ WATERS ABOVE THE SKY: *See Genesis 1.6-7.*

6   by his command they were fixed in
        their places forever,
    and they cannot disobey.[f]

7 Praise the LORD from the earth,
    sea monsters and all ocean depths;
8 lightning and hail, snow and clouds,
    strong winds that obey his command.

9 Praise him, hills and mountains,
    fruit trees and forests;
10 all animals, tame and wild,
    reptiles and birds.

11 Praise him, kings and all peoples,
    princes and all other rulers;
12 girls and young men,
    old people and children too.

13 Let them all praise the name of the
        LORD!
    His name is greater than all others;
    his glory is above earth and heaven.
14 He made his nation strong,
    so that all his people praise him—
    the people of Israel, so dear to him.

Praise the LORD!

A Hymn of Praise

149   Praise the LORD!

    Sing a new song to the LORD;
        praise him in the assembly of his
            faithful people!
2 Be glad, Israel, because of your Creator;
    rejoice, people of Zion, because of
        your king!

---

[f] by his command . . . disobey; *or* he has fixed them in their places
for all time, by a command that lasts forever.

³ Praise his name with dancing;
    play drums and harps in praise of
      him.

⁴ The LORD takes pleasure in his people;
    he honors the humble with victory.
⁵ Let God's people rejoice in their
      triumph
    and sing joyfully all night long.
⁶ Let them shout aloud as they praise
      God,
    with their sharp swords in their
      hands
⁷   to defeat the nations
    and to punish the peoples;
⁸   to bind their kings in chains,
    their leaders in chains of iron;
⁹   to punish the nations as God has
      commanded.
  This is the victory of God's people.

  Praise the LORD!

Praise the LORD!

150   Praise the LORD!

  Praise God in his Temple!
    Praise his strength in heaven!
² Praise him for the mighty things he has
      done.
    Praise his supreme greatness.

³ Praise him with trumpets.
    Praise him with harps and lyres.
⁴ Praise him with drums and dancing.
    Praise him with harps and flutes.
⁵ Praise him with cymbals.
    Praise him with loud cymbals.
⁶ Praise the LORD, all living creatures!

  Praise the LORD!

Praise the LORD! (150.1)

MAPS

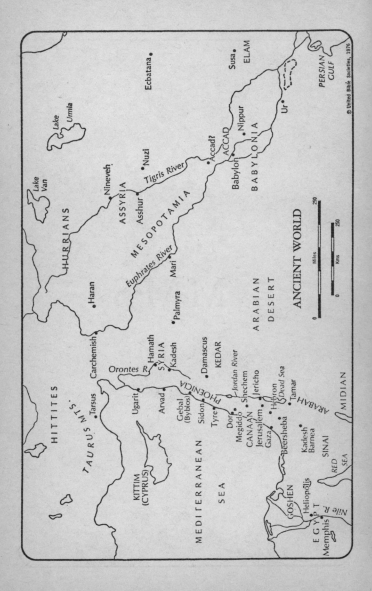

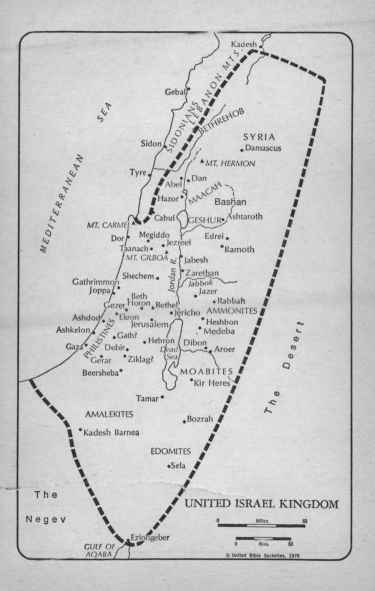

Kadesh

Gebal

SIDONIANS LEBANON MTS.

BETHREHOB

SEA

Sidon

SYRIA

• Damascus

Tyre

▲ MT. HERMON

Abel • Dan

Hazor • MAACAH Bashan

Cabul GESHUR • Ashtaroth

MT. CARMEL

Dor • Megiddo Edrei

Taanach • Jezreel Ramoth

MT. GILBOA ▲ Jabesh

Jordan R.

Shechem • Zarethan

Jabbok

Gathrimmon Jazer

Joppa • Beth Rabbah

Gezer Horon Bethel AMMONITES

Ashdod • Ekron Jericho Heshbon

Ashkelon Jerusalem • Medeba

PHILISTINES • Gath? Hebron Dibon

Gaza Debir Dead • Aroer

Gerar • Ziklag? Sea

Beersheba MOABITES

• Kir Heres

Tamar •

AMALEKITES • Bozrah

• Kadesh Barnea

MEDITERRANEAN

The Desert

EDOMITES

• Sela

The

Negev

UNITED ISRAEL KINGDOM

0 Miles 60

0 Kms 60

© United Bible Societies, 1976

GULF OF
AQABA

Eziongeber